EIGHTH

DAY

OF

CREATION

*Discovering Your
Gifts and Using Them*

EIGHTH DAY OF CREATION

ISBN 1-928717-15-2

Library of Congress catalog card number: 70-175725
Printed in the United States of America
Quotations from the Revised Standard Version of the Bible, copyrighted 1946, 1952, ©1971, 1973 by the Division of Christian Education of the National Council of Churches of Christ in the United States of America; *The New English Bible* © copyright The Delegates of the Oxford University Press and The Syndics of The Cambridge University Press, 1961, 1970, reprinted by permission. Scripture quotations are identified in the text by abbreviations in the conventional form.

Mystery and Manners, Occasional Prose of Flannery O'Connor, selected and edited by Sally and Robert Fitzgerald, copyright © 1957, 1961, 1963, 1964, 1966, 1967, 1969 by the Estate of Mary Flannery O'Connor, copyright 1962 by Flannery O'Connor, copyright © 1961 by Farrar, Straus & Cudahy, Inc. Courtesy of Farrar, Straus & Giroux, Inc.

Cover art, *The Juggler* by Marc Chagall, French, born Russia, 1887–1985, oil on canvas, 1943, 109.9 x 79.1 cm, Gift of Mrs. Gilbert W. Chapman, 1952.1005. © 1992 The Art Institute of Chicago, All Rights Reserved.

Cover design by Brenda M. Palley

Eighth Day of Creation

Creativeness in the world is, as it were, the eighth day of creation.

Nicolas Berdyaev

Be patient toward all that is unsolved in your heart . . . try to love the questions themselves *like locked rooms and like books that are written in a very foreign tongue. Do not now seek the answers, which cannot be given you because you would not be able to live them. And the point is, to live everything. Live the questions now. Perhaps you will then gradually, without noticing it, live along some distant day into the answer.*

Rainer Maria Rilke

Preface

This is another book
which has grown out of the community of The Church
of The Saviour in Washington, D.C. It was originally
written to give guidance to the church's mission
groups working in such varying areas as programs for
the aged, housing for the poor, life-giving structures
for neglected and abandoned children, polycultural
education, leadership training for ghetto youth, and a
coffee house ministry in the inner city.

We are sometimes
asked what accounts for the diversity of our community. In answering we must always speak of the
evoking and exercising of gifts. The classes we give in
our School of Christian Living, the sermons that we
preach, the conferences that we hold are often to help
us with the discovery of our gifts. When we describe

"Church" we like to say that it is a gift-evoking, gift-bearing community—a description based on the conviction that when God calls a person he calls him into the fullness of his own potential. This is why "Church" implies a people; no one enters into a fullness of being except in community with other persons. No community develops the potential of its corporate life unless the gifts of each of its members are evoked and exercised on behalf of the whole community.

Gordon Cosby puts it this way: "When each person is exercising her gift, she becomes an initiating center of life. When we confirm a person's call to this segment of the Church, we say by that confirmation that we will be instruments in calling the person forth in her totality. The one who joins assumes that same responsibility for all the other members of the community. This covenant is implicit in the celebration of commitment of each new member. The Church of the Holy Spirit is full of variety. Sameness and conformity are the demands of alien spirits. No gift is unimportant. There are no lesser gifts. Each is crucial to the proper functioning of the Body; each contributes to the rich diversity needed by the Church for its work within the total organism of humanity. If there are ten people in one of the small groups of the church and each is an evoked person exercising his gift of the Spirit on behalf of the whole, then you have a group with power to attract. People gather around it. They respond to it, they love it, they hate it. Such a group has the power to heal, to liberate, to tackle the demonic systems and structures of society."

And what is the strategy of these small initiating centers of life when they move out into the world? Simply to call forth gifts, to evoke the treasure of personality, to be enablers of others. Part of the frustration and agony of the poor, minority groups, the third world countries, is surely rooted in the fact that they are denied opportunities to use and develop their gifts.

A revolution is going on in the world today that is cutting across lines of class, color, and nationality. It is the revolution of those all over the world who are in on the secret of gifts. At the heart of it is the gospel, but the Church cannot assert this in the traditional words of the faith because of a noisy piety that failed to become embodied in authentic life styles. In this revolution one gift is neither superior nor inferior to another. The recognition dawns that the exercising of gifts is wrapped up with our needs which mesh with corresponding needs in the world. The Peace Mission Group in our church, in the course of its efforts to help the congregation attain a fuller understanding of the meaning of Christian nonviolence, learns to deal with its own violent responses to life. Those who move among the poor discover and confront their own conflicts with money and possessions. I write a book and find in its pages answers to my own questions. We exercise our gifts and learn that there is a mysterious law of reciprocity at work in the universe.

As the artist discovers that there is a direct relationship between the inner and outer forms of material, so we discover that creativity in our inner lives has a direct relationship to creativity in the world. We can never be in the world only as its benefactors. This does not make for authentic relationship. All that we genuinely do is very personal and calls into being our own personality. The covenant of the Church to call forth gifts is extended to the whole of humankind. I say to the world, "I will be an instrument of God in the continuing act of creation," and the world fulfills in me its side of the covenant. It brings forth in me the new creation.

In the end, we have to say that the exercising of gifts has to do with love, which is a reciprocal relationship. We are addressed by love, and we love. The two exercises in this book are preparation for love and so they are very difficult, because to love is very difficult. Anything that I have written can be read in one sitting, but the exercises — they may take months and years to do. They require a reflective mind and a contemplative heart. The selections that follow both exercises suggest areas for exploration, give encouragement, raise questions, point out paths. Read a few each day meditatively. Treat them as guides or teachers, but then leave

them and enter into that still point at the center of
your own life and there ask your questions and wait
for your answers.

Try to reserve a half-
hour each day for this work, preferably at the same
time and in the same place. You may want to keep a
journal in which you write anything that comes to
mind during this time. Do not censor any of your
thoughts or try to record them in orderly fashion.
Write your journal as notes to yourself. Give special
attention to the images that cross the screen of your
mind. Another age called them visions. They are
much more important than we have ever guessed.
Ask their meaning. Then wait, and watch, and listen.

Many write to us and
ask for materials that will assist them in their individual and group life. The pages that follow reflect
the kind of search our community is engaged in and
the questions that we ponder in our solitude. Certainly our knowledge of gifts and creativity is incomplete, a subject to be pondered and worked through in
this and every church community. We are just beginning to ask the important questions.

For me to complete a
book requires a gift-evoking community. This volume, the previously published *Our Many Selves*[1], and
Search for Silence[2] form a trilogy which never could

have been done without the gracious help of friends. Dorothy Devers gave generous editorial assistance. Countless sentences are better for her touch. Gordon Cosby is the one who gives inspiration and leadership to the whole concept of evoking gifts in our community. Other patron saints were John Tuohey, Mary Jo Cook and Kathleen Murphy.

And then there is that large company of those who were not offended because I was lost in the pages of a book. Among the real costs of exercising a gift are feelings of guilt for all the things one saw to do and left undone; but even more for gentle thoughts one did not take the time to speak; and then for the knowledge that a work that bears a single name should have written across it a hundred.

Eighth Day of Creation

Gifts and Creativity

Somewhere I heard a story about Michelangelo's pushing a huge piece of rock down a street. A curious neighbor sitting lazily on the porch of his house called to him and inquired why he labored so over an old piece of stone. Michelangelo is reported to have answered, "Because there is an angel in that rock that wants to come out."

This story comes to mind when I think about the gifts or talents given to each of us. Every person has the task of releasing angels by shaping and transfiguring the raw materials that lie about her so that they become houses and machinery and pictures and bridges. How we do this—how we "build the earth," to use Teilhard de Chardin's phrase—is determined by the discovery and the use of our gifts.

Because our gifts carry us out into the world and make us participants in life, the uncovering of them is one of the most important tasks confronting any one of us. When we talk about being true to ourselves—being the persons we are intended to be—we are talking about gifts. We cannot be ourselves unless we are true to our gifts. When we talk about vocation, whether we are artists or engineers, we are talking about gifts. In a discussion about commitment, we are on the same subject for the place of our concrete involvement is determined by our gifts. Serious reflection on almost any aspect of our lives leads into a consideration of gifts.

Whenever we struggle with what we are to do in life, we are struggling to uncover our talent or gift. For many it is a lifetime struggle. Few people feel good about the jobs they hold. The vast number have no sense of being in the right place and are always looking for something else without knowing what it is. The statement is often made to personnel directors and friends, "I want a job working with people." They do not say, "I like people and I have equipped myself to be a nurse, or a teacher." Most of us do not have that much understanding of gifts. We respond in a very general way as almost anyone could, "I would like to work with people." Every serious artist or researcher working at his lonely trade is aware that, in the service of his gifts, one of the sacrifices he makes is the company of others, or at least the development of a capacity for relationship if this is lacking. Actually the statement that we "would like to work with people" could be an evasion to prevent our dealing specifically with the matter of our peculiar gifts.

We ask to know the will of God without guessing that his will is written into our very beings. We perceive that will when we discern our gifts. Our obedience and surrender to God are in large part our obedience and surrender to our gifts. This is the message wrapped up in the parable of the talents. Our gifts are on loan. We are responsible for spending them in the world, and we will be held accountable. Though it may seem that God leaves us and is not concerned with what we do with our lives, the parable makes it clear that this is not the case. Even though we feel he is away a long time—the absent God—we perceive his presence in the consequences of our actions.

As with all the parables in the Gospels, this is a story of the inner life and, like everything in Scripture, it is not there to address some minority group, but all of us. Like many of the parables this one is full of joy and good news. To those of us who keep comparing ourselves with someone else comes the word that it is unimportant how many talents anyone has—two or five. If we use those we have, our lives will expand and our capacity will double. A message that sounds throughout the New Testament is here again in the story of the talents: she who loses her life will find it. Cast your bread upon the waters and it will come back tenfold.

This parable says nothing about equality of gifts or equality of distribution, but it does promise the same reward to all—the joy of being a creator. The one who uses well the two talents hears the same pronouncement as the one who uses well the five, ". . . I will set you over much; enter into the joy of your master" (Matt. 25: 21,23, RSV).

As a rule, however, our attention is not caught by those in the parable who are exercising their gifts in freedom and joy. It is the one-talent man who captures our imagination and moves us to compassion. His cautious, protective measure seems very reasonable—"I was afraid, and I went and hid your talent in the ground" (Matt. 25: 25, RSV).

We can sympathize with that. So buried away are our gifts that we do not know what they are. When the Scripture goes on to say, "... cast the worthless servant into the outer darkness; there men will weep and gnash their teeth," we rise up in protest. How horribly unjust! What kind of God have we, anyway? And yet the experience of this Scripture is in our own lives. If we do not use our gifts, we know an anguish of spirit that is not relieved by the explanation that we had parents who did not listen to us, teachers who demanded conformity, and structures that made us feel inferior. When the man in the story responds, "I knew you to be a hard man, reaping where you did not sow, and gathering where you did not winnow . . . ," he explains why he is afraid, revealing at the same time his terror of authority figures as those who are out to take what is not theirs. The Scripture does not argue about how any of us experiences the world; rather it holds us all responsible for our lives and what we are doing with them.

Once more, Jesus has told a story that we can understand—a story to shake us out of our lethargy. The parable puts us in touch with our own pain. In unmistakable terms are spelled out the consequences of not uncovering and spending our gifts—our failure to be creators. But our suffering can be our hope if it impels us to give attention to what is crushed and dying in us, and wants to live and bear fruit.

When we deny our gifts, we blaspheme against the Holy Spirit whose action is to call forth gifts. In every person is the creation story. Since the first day of our beginning, the Spirit has brooded over the formless, dark void of our lives, calling us into fullness of being through our gifts. And that same Spirit gives us the responsibility of investing those gifts in the continuing creation of the world. Our gifts are the signs of our commissioning, the conveyors of our human-divine love, the receptacles of our own transforming, creative power.

A primary purpose of the Church is to help us discover and develop our gifts and, in the face of our fears, to hold us accountable for them so that we can enter into the joy of creating. The major obligation of the Church to children is to enjoy them and to listen to them so that each can grow according to the design which is written into the being of each and emerges only under the care and warmth of another life. One of the reasons we experience so much difficulty with our gifts is that parents have thought their chief function in life is to feed, clothe, and educate the young. However, their really important ministry is to listen to their children and enable them to uncover the special blueprint that is theirs. There is one line in Scripture that will instruct us in these matters: "But Mary treasured up all these things and pondered over them" (Luke 2:19, NEB).

Every child's life gives forth hints and signs of the way that it is to go. The parent that knows how to meditate stores away these hints and signs and ponders over them. We are to treasure the intimations of the future that the child gives to us so that, instead of unconsciously putting blocks in the way, we help that life to fulfill its destiny. This is not an easy way to follow. Instead of telling our children what they should do and become, we must be humble before their wisdom, believing that in them and not in us is the secret that they need to discover.

Eric Hoffer tells a story about a Bavarian peasant woman who cared for him after his mother died and during the years that he was blind: "And this woman, this Martha took care of me. She was a big woman, with a small head. And this woman, this Martha, must have really loved me, because those eight years of blindness are in my mind as a happy time. I remember a lot of talk and laughter. I must have talked a great deal, because Martha used to say again and again, 'You remember you said this, you remember you said that. . . .' She remembered everything I said, and all my life I've had the feeling that what I think and what I say are worth remembering. She gave me that . . . ."[1]

One of the reasons we have difficulty identifying our gifts is that we have had no one to listen to us or even to look at us. In Thornton Wilder's play, *Our Town,* after Emily has died she chooses to return to her home and observe the day of her twelfth birthday. As she watches the day unfold, she becomes painfully aware that no one really notices what is going on. Finally she cries, "I can't, I can't go on. It goes so fast. We don't have time to look at one another."

Very few of us have had a listening, seeing person in our lives. We do not hear what others—not even our children—are saying because we, ourselves, have had no one to hear us. We do not have the feeling that what we think and what we say are important.

Many of us make this confession to one another in the small groups of The Church of The Saviour when we struggle to identify and exercise our gifts. Such confession helps to dispel one's illusion of being the only one who lacks confidence and needs confirmation. We begin to see that our need is everyone's need and that the person who looks so assured and confident and collected is hardly ever feeling that way. We wear masks for each other to hide how uncertain and afraid we are. If we think about it, we know that the other did not give us the confirmation we were seeking because she was too busy trying to find confirmation for herself. As for us, we could not answer her plea, so concerned were we with our own place in the scheme of things.

When this happens in a group, we do not have Christian community or any other kind of community. We may be sitting in a circle in the same room, but each of us is living in a separate world revolving around self. And what we hear and see is in terms of ourselves, which is to see or hear hardly at all. To be a person in community one must both give and receive, confirm and be confirmed. The Christian Church comes into being as we come to know our gifts and help others to know theirs.

At the point of our gifts we see how utterly related prayer is to our whole existence. The silence of prayer is the silence of listening. Because there was no person who listened to us does not mean that all is lost. We can learn to listen to ourselves, and we can learn to listen to one another. What we discover in the prayer of silence can be used as we listen at the altar of our own lives. In our wishes, small urgings, dreams, and fantasies, we are given intimations of the way we are to go. It is our way alone and cannot be learned by reading books or listening to scholars or following others. We can learn our way only by taking seriously the sign that we see and the small voice that we hear. These we must treasure up in our hearts and ponder over. The code we are to decipher is written into our genes and sent out to us, as it were, from the core of our beings.

Whenever I think that there is a design written into each life—a blueprint that can be known—I am reminded of those rubbings that artists make of stone carvings on buildings and tombstones. I imagine what it would be like if we could have a rubbing of our lives, a map that would show us where we are headed and how to get there. Sometimes I think I would like that. We would have no blind alleys. Every road would be a royal road; but there would be no mystery, no work to do, no obstacles to overcome, and we would not need one another. After all, what are blind alleys but God's way of telling us that we missed the reading of a sign and to go back and start again. And what are our hopes and "sighing after" but rubbings of something deep and hidden in us.

We listen for the signs and hints in other lives in the very same way that we listen for them in our own. One aspect of our preliminary preparation for small group meetings in my own community is meditation on the lives of the members of the group so that we can begin to hear what each is saying and, by our listening, become an evoker of gifts. A person who listens helps us overcome our timidity and pulls out of us all kinds of amazing insights.

In a nonthreatening atmosphere where there is warmth and acceptance and someone to receive what we have to give, creativity begins to flow. Those congregations that punctuate the sermons of their ministers with "amens" are giving them untold encouragement. We have a woman in our congregation who nods her head in approval through all the sermons we unseasoned laypersons give. Her encouragement does not make us think we are better than we are. It simply enables us to do what we do as well as we can. Actors affirm the same thing. They insist that their performances differ because audiences vary, drawing a variety of qualities from the performers.

In one sense the encouragement that we give to one another is of utmost importance. Creativity puts us in touch with our divinity so that Christ may be formed in us, and we may be in the service of gifts in ourselves and in others. As the prophecy of Isaiah was fulfilled in Jesus, so it will be in us: "He will not snap off the broken reed, nor snuff out the smouldering wick" (Matt. 12: 20, NEB).

While the prophecy must work out in us if we are to be the Church, we will be in trouble if we have to have a nodding head and an "amen" to all our efforts. Another serious injunction is given in Philippians. After describing the love and encouragement and compassion that we are to give each other, the author points out a more solitary way—the way of the Cross that is also ours, "You must work out your own salvation in fear and trembling; for it is God who works in you, inspiring both the will and the deed, for his own chosen purpose" (Phil. 2:12-13, NEB). The same thought occurs in other places in Scripture. Whereas we are to help one another carry heavy loads, "everyone has his own proper burden to bear" (Gal. 6:5, NEB).

The act of creation is always a solitary one. Others can encourage us to create. They cannot create for us. The man of one talent needs the same courage as the man of ten. I once thought that only great gifts were exercised without continual confirmation. Darwin's father may have tried to impose on him first the career of doctor and then that of clergyman, but unlike our fathers he could not succeed, so great was Darwin's affinity with nature and his aptitude for discovery.

Surely, I reasoned, it must be the magnitude of their gifts that enables artists and scientists and inventors to go on producing when they are rejected and scorned by their contemporaries. Now I am not so sure that the greatness of the talent has any direct relation to the degree of persistence with which it is developed. When I become aware of my own gifts and give my attention to communicating what is in me—my own truth, as it were—I have the experience of growing toward wholeness. I am working out God's "chosen purpose," and I am no longer dependent on what others think and how they respond. The experience itself is confirming. The response of others can give me pleasure or pain, but it cannot keep me from the act of creating. I am content to be nobody because I know that in the important inner realm of the Spirit I am somebody. Through the exercising of my gifts I am in the process of realizing and communicating my own uncommon self.

We cannot listen and speak and work out of our own centers and at the same time give our attention to weighing whether or not others are approving of us. But the fact is that probably no one— not even the saint—operates continually from her innermost self. One of the certain signs that we are at the periphery of our lives is our beginning to wonder whether or not what we are doing will be pleasing to others. Whenever we begin to act and produce with the approval of others in mind, there comes the haunting possibility that we will not live up to their actual or imagined expectations. To the degree that this feeling takes over we abandon ourselves, and spontaneity and creativity die in us. We enter into the sin of judging our own works, of deciding what is good and what is bad, when our only task is to be faithful over what we have—to do the best we can with it and to leave the judgment to God. We do not have to be better than others, or live up to their expectations, or fulfill their demands. When the beggar at the gate of the temple called Beautiful asked alms of Peter and John, Peter said to him, "I have no silver and gold, but I give you what I have. . . ." (Acts 3: 6, RSV). We meditate on Scripture so that we can be liberated from false strivings and give something of our own to the world.

One of the fears that binds so many is the fear of rejection. We have our gifts wrapped up and buried away because we are afraid they will not be received. Our gifts can be buried so deep that we do not even know what they are. This is why so much attention must be given to evoking and using gifts. The teaching, preaching ministry of the church is to help a person discover the gifts to be used in creating one's own life, in building the Church of Jesus Christ, and in healing the world so that each of us can be "the repairer of the breach, the restorer of streets to dwell in" (Isa .58: 12,RSV)

Almost from the time a person comes in touch with The Church of The Saviour she hears about gifts and is confronted with the question, "What are your gifts?" Another way of asking that question is, "What is your call?"—so often we come to appreciate our gifts by knowing our calls. All the mission groups[2] of The Church of The Saviour come into existence in response to a person's call. For example, someone may want to work in the area of curing drug addiction, or in some phase of education. If the call is sounded so that it comes as good news to others and they want to work in the accomplishment of certain goals, then we have a new mission group. And when a new group comes into existence, one of its first tasks is to identify the gifts of each of its members so that every person is exercising a gift on behalf of the group. Each of the groups has a moderator, a spiritual director, a teacher, a pastor prophet, a shepherd, and an activist or plowman. Also, each person, with the help of the group members, names a gift that can be used in performing the tasks the group has defined for itself.

Bonhoeffer in *Life Together* says, "A community which allows unemployed members to exist within it will perish because of them. It will be well, therefore, if every member receives a definite task to perform for the community, that he may know in hours of doubt that he, too, is not useless and unusable."[3] In our own community

Gordon Cosby[4] is the person who constantly reminds us of this. He believes with a passion the New Testament teaching that " . . . grace was given to each of us according to the measure of Christ's gift . . . he gave gifts to men. . . . And his gifts were that some should be apostles, some prophets, some evangelists, some pastors and teachers, for the equipment of the saints, for the work of the ministry, for building up the body of Christ." (Eph. 4: 7, 12, RSV). Cosby says that the Scriptures on gifts that we find in Romans, Corinthians, and Ephesians contain spiritual dynamite. "If we will take them seriously, they will set off a revolution in the churches that will bring in a whole new age of the Spirit."

To be in earnest about these Scriptures is a costly business, for they have to do with call and gifts and creativity, and our reply is that of the one-talented man—we are scared. Sometimes it takes a year or two for us to identify the gifts in our groups. The "new age of the Spirit" is not going to come without birth pangs. And perhaps those birth pangs will be our willingness to struggle first to discover what our gifts are and then to risk investing them in an unsure world where there is no certain return. If we could be confident of success and know in advance that someone would eventually say that we could share in the creator's joy, we would have no need for faith. But it is not the good works that we do or the things that we make, it is our faith that saves us, and this is not easy to know.

In the small groups in my church community the element of fear plays a big part in the struggle to identify our gifts. We try out one gift timidly, find out that it is not right, and continue trying out others until we find the one that we feel good about. We cannot fool ourselves for long about what we are to do. Somewhere deep down in us is stored the secret, and when we are digging in the wrong place, we know it. The secret wants to be discovered and will not let us go in peace a way that is not ours.

On one occasion I was in a group where everyone except for a gracious and lovely woman had a gift identified. When we went on a weekend retreat, she told us the first evening that she was uneasy because she did not know what her gift was. She was an appealing person whose very presence was a gift. In one way and another we told her that it seemed that her gift was just to be among us and to do what she was doing. "For after all," we said, "a person is in her very being a gift."

We have discovered, however, that while this is true, we do not experience ourselves as gift until we are engaged in the act of creating. The confirmation of a person as gift acknowledges what is obvious, but it does not give enough attention to what is not as evident—the unknown potential in a person that can be brought into existence only through the exercising of gifts. We cannot use our gifts without having unknown chords in us played upon in a whole range of effects that bring us alive.

Our group member found unsatisfactory the response that she, herself, was gift. She could not understand this and felt that she lacked worth as a person because she did not know her gifts. Members of the group suggested one gift after the other that she might exercise on behalf of the mission, but while each one suggested rang true for us and we might have confirmed her in a number of ministries, no suggestion connected with anything deep in her.

One can have a similar experience trying to interpret another person's dream or struggling to find out the meaning of one's own dream. When the time has come for a person to know what a dream is saying and the signs of his dream are interpreted so that he is in on a part of his life that has been unknown to him, all his feelings confirm the interpretation. Whereas, if the signs and symbols of a dream have been wrongly read or not interpreted at all, feelings can range from deadness to rage.

One of the most vivid examples we have of a person's struggle to understand the buried longings of his life is Nebuchadnezzar's search for someone to interpret his recurring dreams. The story begins with the opening sentence of the second chapter of Daniel: "In the second year of his reign Nebuchadnezzar had dreams, and his mind was so troubled that he could not sleep." Usually we have to be deeply disturbed to be concerned about our dreams, and then we are willing to go to great lengths and pay all kinds of money to discover their meaning, a fact that is always bewildering to peaceful sleepers. Nebuchadnezzar summoned the experts and professionals of his day—the magicians, exorcists, sorcerers, and Chaldeans. In his anguish he threatened them with death if they did not interpret his dream. Out of fear the "wise men" conspired to save their own lives rather than risk helping the distraught king, and answered, "Nobody on earth can tell your majesty what you wish to know . . . .What your majesty requires of us is too hard" (Dan. 2: 10, 11, NEB).

The king was not fooled. He knew that his question had an answer and that the answer was essential for the living of his life. In anger and despair he decreed that his counselors should be executed. When Daniel, whose special gift was to interpret dreams and visions, heard of the sentence, he begged the king to allow him a certain length of time at the end of which he would interpret the dream. This granted, he went home and told the whole story to Hananiah, Mishael, and Azariah, his own small community of believers, so that they would pray with him. Then in a vision Daniel was given the secret of the dream that could not be fathomed by a purely scientific, analytical approach. In essence he told Nebuchadnezzar that in heaven was a god who wanted him to know the interpretation of his dream and to understand the thoughts which had entered his mind. "He reveals deep mysteries; he knows what lies in darkness" (Dan. 2: 22, NEB).

Woven through Daniel's long explanation of the symbols and signs of the dream is the message that Nebuchadnezzar's kingdom couldn't last. The king, a man given to intense fury, might have had Daniel killed for such an interpretation, but the news rang true. Nebuchadnezzar had known it with a large part of him already. It was the basis of an anxiety that he could not understand. Now instead of being a vague knowledge, hidden away where he could not come to terms with it, it was out in the open.

More than that, Daniel, a prophet and interpreter of dreams, was also an evangelist and brought him the good news of Jesus Christ—the Kingdom of Heaven is at hand. His precise words were, ". .. the God of heaven will establish a kingdom which shall never be destroyed; that kingdom shall never pass to another people; it shall shatter and make an end of all these kingdoms, while it shall itself endure for ever" (Dan. 2:44, NEB).

The kingdoms that any of us build are destructible and are always under threat. No wonder we feel so vulnerable, so easily shaken and disturbed by feelings that we cannot understand. No one whose life is not in touch with a transcendent order can possibly exercise his gifts with abandonment. It is only when our lives quicken to the news of the Advent of another Kingdom and we invest ourselves in its coming that we can be sure what we do endures forever. For all his shortcomings, Nebuchadnezzar in this instance was aware enough of his feelings to know that they had a message of importance for him.

Though Nebuchadnezzar's story seems far removed, I was reminded of it by the woman on our retreat who was asking for an interpretation of her feelings. She did not threaten to banish us from her sight, but she told us in her own way that we had misread the signs of her life. Even though she had not been able to identify her gift, she knew we were wrong. We had named the gifts that were obvious to her as well as to us, but she was seeking to know something more hidden.

One reason for difficulty in our lives is that others have confirmed in us the obvious or what they, themselves, wanted to see. To please them, or to get ahead, or to make more money—we then developed those gifts, meanwhile putting aside and forgetting the gifts which were neither so evident nor so valued by others. If our unused gifts have any strength or power of their own, they cry out for recognition—to be given a name. They are not only disturbers of our sleep; they make our days uneasy.

As Daniel had asked his prayer group to pray with him, our group member asked us to pray with her so that she could discover the gift that she was to use on behalf of the mission. In the closing session of the retreat she told us that in her imagination she had role-played all the gifts we had suggested, but that none of them had felt right. Out of her praying, however, had come the feeling that she had a gift for intercessory prayer. She knew that it mattered to her that other people were praying for her that weekend, and she began to know that she would enjoy praying for others. She had the conviction that her prayers would count and even began to think that she might have something to say to those who were deeply questioning the value of intercessory prayer.

The group had no difficulty in confirming her as an intercessor. Confirmation of her gift did not mean that the rest of us would give up our prayers of intercession for one another and the group and its mission, but it did mean that we now had a person who would spend more time at the work of intercession. Perhaps hers would always be a hidden work; on the other hand she might become a teacher. In any case, if the parable of the talents is true, her capacity for intercession would grow.

Confirmation of a gift also carries a responsibility to others. Part of this is to hold the person accountable for his gift. Again this is in the parable. How does another person know that we have taken what he has said with any seriousness if we do not ask what he has done with his gift? The reason our groups go through the process of naming our gifts and making explicit our covenant is so that we can grow in responsibility and move toward authentic freedom. The person who is seriously interested in investing his life does not perceive the time of accounting as something to be anticipated with dread, but as a caring which supports and encourages him in what he wants to do.

Gifts that are accepted with difficulty into awareness can very easily slip out of consciousness. They need to be remembered and tended. Confirmation of a gift by the members of a mission group means a willingness to be obedient to the person at the point of her gift. This is the basis of the lines of authority in a group. If a person names her gift and is willing to be responsible in the area of her gift, those who confirm her recognize her authority. They have listened to her and heard her gift as an articulation of her life.

In our hearing lies our obedience. Just as the person's hearing of his own gift brings him under its authority—obedient to what it will ask of him—so the community's hearing of that gift brings its members under obedience. The gift is a gift of the Holy Spirit. The Spirit calls it forth and the power of the Spirit becomes visible in its exercising. The Spirit-filled community is a community where each person is exercising his gift or gifts on behalf of the whole.

One of the first gifts that we name in a group is the gift of prior or moderator. No group comes into existence unless there is a person who has this gift and is willing to exercise it. The prior has many responsibilities, but perhaps the chief call upon him is to be an enabler or evoker of gifts. His special responsibility is to see that every person is either exercising his gift or grappling with the naming of it. He is, of course, not alone in this charge any more than he is alone in his other responsibilities.

The person with the gift of intercession prays daily for every single person in the group that each one may discover her gift and exercise it in freedom. The pastor-prophet of the group will comfort, encourage, and challenge members of the group as they try to use their gifts. In a sense, the members of the small groups of the church are the patrons of gifts—patron being defined as "one chosen, named, or honored as a special guardian, protector, supporter, or the like."

A patron is much more fundamental than we have thought to the discovery and emergence of gifts. Very few people creatively and happily engaged in their work can look back without seeing behind the evolving of their gifts the faces of their patron saints. It is probably just as well

that we have not always named these saints, for if
Petru Dumitriu is right, we would lead them into the
temptation of pride and vanity and they would have
to go instantly into hiding. As it is now, the churches
are endangered because they do not know the necessity of saints for the emergence of gifts and flow of
creativity.

Two reasons for the
poverty of patrons in the world are our jealousy and
envy. These emotions lie close to us all and are in
evidence when we have an unfolding life. The more
full of promise a life is the more it is apt to evoke un-
comfortable responses in others. If a community is to
exist at all, it must learn to deal openly and creatively
with feelings of jealousy and envy.

Many of the communes
that young people in the 60's began with such high
hopes did not survive because of rivalry and jealousy
among the members. The church is not exempt from
having to struggle with these emotions if it wants to
be a genuine community with structures for freedom
and wholeness. My guess is that we have so little
real community in our churches because we have chosen to keep life on a polite, superficial plane rather
than suffer the agony of coping with the problems
that arise when we commit ourselves to any close covenant relationship. These problems become com-
pounded when the community is engaged in the
creation of structures that bring out and develop the
gifts of its members. As long as we keep our discus-

sion of the "calling forth of gifts," which is the term we use at The Church of The Saviour, on a theoretical plane, we experience the concept as an exciting one, even challenging. When we begin actually to put it into practice, we encounter some of the difficulties involved. Certainly high on the list are both jealousy and envy, which must be raised into full consciousness if we are to move through them to actualize our own gifts, to become patrons of gifts, and maybe even patron saints.

Neither the Old nor the New Testament makes any effort to minimize the problem for the community. The Genesis story brings it clearly into focus when it discusses the gifts of the brothers of the first family: "The Lord received Abel and his gift with favour; but Cain and his gift he did not receive. Cain was very angry and his face fell. Then the Lord said to Cain, 'Why are you so angry and cast down?'" (Gen. 4:4,6, NEB).

The question seems like an easy one for Cain to answer. After all, he was a tiller of the soil and had brought the fruit of his labor as a gift to the Lord. Is there anyone who would not feel rejected under these circumstances? God did not wait for Cain to answer the question. He went right on to say, "If you do well, you are accepted; if not, sin is a demon crouching at the door. It shall be eager for you, and you will be mastered by it" (Gen. 4:7, NEB).

35

We can only deduce that Cain was holding back. He had not yet discovered his true vocation. The warning was that if he did not apply himself to the task of finding himself, his jealous feelings would take over and rule him.

A similar theme runs through many of the stories that we remember from the Old Testament. The brothers Jacob and Esau turn the envious eye on each other. Then there is Joseph, outfitted in color and style, confident of his future and certain that he is born to rule, he stirs his brothers to jealousy by telling them dreams that constellate all their fears about his favored place in the scheme of things. These are stories of the young, starting out in life under all kinds of pressure in the modern, rapidly changing society of that time.

We talk about violent change in our life situation, but what could be more radical than to be catapulted out of a quiet, secluded garden where all one's needs were provided into a world of unlimited possibility where nothing was known? Cain and Abel could not have escaped absorbing some of the anxiety of the parents. Surely as humankind and individuals grow older they gain a heart of wisdom. But no. Envy and jealousy—sin, in other words—are not the disease of older civilizations or the untried young. The words spoken to Cain outside the garden come true centuries later in the life of King Saul, who in his middle years is mastered by his envy of the young man David. The heart of the story is in a few passages: "At the homecoming of the army when David returned from the slaughter of the Philistines, the women came out from all the cities of Israel to look on, and the dancers came out to meet King Saul with tambourines, singing, and dancing. The women as they made merry sang to one another: 'Saul made havoc among thousands but David among tens of thousands.' Saul was furious, and the words rankled. He said,'They have given David tens of thousands and me only thousands; what more can they do but make him king?' From that day forward Saul kept a jealous eye on David" (1 Sam. 18:6-9, NEB).

Neither age nor success in themselves take care of the problems of jealousy and envy. Because the old and the successful have kingdoms to think about, they are in a position to be even more threatened by the emerging gifts of others. The New Testament opens with the same theme that we find in the opening pages of the Old Testament. This time it is a king who fears the potential wrapped in the life of a baby. Thirty-three years later jealousy and envy succeed in mobilizing the powers and forces that seek to eliminate all the threatening possibilities of that life.

In that first mission group of twelve—up until the very end of his ministry with them—Jesus is helping the small church to deal with problems of rivalry and jealousy. The same question that is raised in the halls of government and in the established church is asked also in the intimate circle, "Who amongst us will be greatest?" In the Gospel of John the last recorded conversation of Jesus is one in which he is trying to focus the attention of Peter on his own destiny. He has just disclosed to him the manner in which he, Peter, will die, and then added, "Follow me." If ever there was a time for Peter's attention to be riveted on his own life, this was it, but the account says: "Peter looked round, and saw the disciple whom Jesus loved following—the one who at supper had leaned back close to him to ask the question, 'Lord, who is it that will betray you?' When he caught sight of him, Peter asked, 'Lord, what will happen to him?' Jesus said, 'If it should be my will that he wait until I come, what is it to you? Follow me' " (John 21:20-22, NEB).

At times it is appropriate for us to compare ourselves with others to help understand our own task. Comparisons also help us to determine the evils in society and gain an understanding of inequalities that come through discriminatory practices or the misuse of power. This creative use of comparison enables us to redress wrongs. Envy makes another kind of comparison. Envy does not have one's self as the subject of attention. It makes the other person all important—his gifts, successes, and achievements, what he does and what happens to him. As long as my energy is spent in watching the life of another, I do not have it to give to the consideration and realization of my own potential. The gold that we spend in one place we cannot spend in another. Also, if I am threatened by a person's gifts, I do not want to see them emerge into any kind of prominence. I may even go so far as to put obstacles in my imagined rival's way and make things hard for him.

As one person in a mission group confessed, "I wanted to be the administrator, but at the same time I didn't want the responsibility that went with it. I couldn't say yes when it was suggested to me; at the same time I knew I was going to make it hard for anyone else to fill that role." This confession was the beginning of his being able to give attention to the creating of his own life. It also helped the group to deal more honestly with resistances to leadership. As contemplative prayer has a direct bearing on the unfolding of our gifts, so has confession.

In his book *The Ways of the Will*, Leslie H. Farber has a chapter entitled, "The Faces of Envy," which is extremely profitable reading and concludes with this statement: "It seems to me that the most pressing concern, for the patient or for ourselves, in regard to so damaging and disturbing an affliction as envy, is not so much to ponder when, or even why, it may originally come into being, as to discover it now where it is, to outwit its distractions and disguises, to measure its fear of being called by name."[5]

Helpful in dealing with our envy or jealousy is the knowledge that these feelings are giving us clear warning that we have abandoned ourselves. If we keep our attention focused on the other person, we only increase our pain and anxiety. Envy is a symptom of lack of appreciation of our own uniqueness and self-worth. Each of us has something to give that no one else has to give. When we can stay at home with ourselves and give what we have, we will not be threatened by what others have to give.

If our own envy keeps us from the work of uncovering our gifts, so does our fear of the envy of others. Sometimes, all unconsciously we live our lives in such a way as not to gain the attention of others. We dread the possibility that someone else might want what we have so we take our gifts and hide them away. We cannot protect ourselves or others from envy by pretending that we are not the possessors of gifts. As we find courage to confess our envy, so we must find courage to confess our gifts. Only the exercising of our own gifts enables us to become patrons of gifts in others and to participate in the coming of that new day when "Bonded and knit together by every constituent joint, the whole frame grows through the due activity of each part, and builds itself up in love" (Eph. 4: 16, NEB).

William F. Lynch in his book, *Images of Hope,*[6] gives three important steps in moving beyond envy to freedom. The first is the recognition of being envious; the second, a deep acceptance of the feeling; and the third, its mastery and self-control. The first two steps, without which the third is never reached, are very difficult because both envy and jealousy are considered such unacceptable and inferior feelings that the confession of them seems impossible. The shame connected with these feelings is so great that we disguise them from ourselves. If we do recognize them, it is usually because the intensity of our pain stabs us awake; then we feel alone and humiliated, rejecting ourselves, unable to confide in anyone, unless our sufferings finally drive us to seek help. Most of us, however, do not suffer this much, and so we save ourselves from having to confess our humanness. We handle our feelings by withdrawing from threatening situations. All that we know is that we are uneasy in groups. We never ask the question, why? If we do not build walls around ourselves, we build them around others, or we may be more aggressive, and undermine in devious ways the enemies of our peace. We say that we belong to a gift-evoking community and do not guess why the gifts are not evoked in ourselves or in others.

The identifying of gifts brings to the fore another large issue in our lives—the issue of commitment. Somehow if I name my gift and it is confirmed, I cannot "hang loose" in the same way. I would much rather be committed to God in the abstract than be committed to Him at the point of my gifts. Becoming specific detracts from the spiritual purity of my communion with the Lord. As with visions, so with gifts, I have once again the job of uniting in myself the opposites—heaven and earth.

The level of earth brings into consideration disagreeable aspects of life such as accountability. Can you imagine tying up something so earthy as accountability with something so lofty as gifts? Jesus came to set men free and here I am in a community that wants to put me on the hook of accountability. But it is even worse than I imagine. When one really becomes practical about gifts, they spell out responsibility and sacrifice.

If I develop one gift, it means that other gifts will not be used. Doors will close on a million lovely possibilities. I will become a painter or a doctor only if denial becomes a part of my picture of reality. Commitment at the point of my gifts means that I must give up being a straddler. Somewhere in the deeps of me I know this. Life will not be the smorgasbord I have made it, sampling and tasting here and there. My commitment will give me an identity. When asked who I am, I will be reminded that the answer lies in the exercising of my gifts. I will have to answer, "I am a writer." "I am a teacher." But I do not like the sound of this. I do not want to be boxed in. "As for me," says the evasive one, "I would rather keep the quest for who I am on a more spiritual plane."

A friend of mine tells a story about commitment and identity that is helpful for me to remember when I find myself resisting the naming of my gifts. He had attended a variety of churches over a long period of time. "I could tell you," he said, "what was good about them and what they would do well to change. I did not think too much about my own commitment. I knew that I was 'for Jesus,' but then I was also for a lot of other good things, like equal job opportunities and poverty programs. When the Poor People's March on Washington took place in 1967, I was pleased to be a part of the crowd, though I was careful to avoid carrying any of the banners or signs that my church had made for I was much too cautious in those days to be publicly identified with what those signs said. I was standing off to the side—like a camp follower—when the crowds began to move toward the Lincoln Memorial. A contagious, happy feeling of excitement was in the air and suddenly I was caught up in it. We were moving down toward the memorial eight abreast when I looked up and saw the TV cameras! I looked around quickly and found an excuse to get out of the path of their lenses. I was in the march for as long as it didn't count, but when I was about to be identified with it, I slipped out."

When the day was over, he was no longer feeling good. A day that had begun with his knowing a sense of aliveness and buoyancy ended with his feeling "half a person." When he reflected on the march and relived the moments of his desertion, they became—as Peter's betrayal had for him—the turning point that moved him toward commitment. Whenever a person becomes committed, she is willing to say who she is and who her friends are, and even to lay down her life for them. Our commitment gives us identity and makes us whole. We are saved from hiding who we are.

The struggle with commitment is not settled once and for all. New opportunities and different stages in life call on us to use different gifts and to make different contributions. As Peter Drucker said in a conversation, "Here I am 58 and I still don't know what I'm going to do when I grow up."[7]

One evidence of an evasion that is used from time to time is an exaggerated concern about where other people are in their lives and about how much they are willing to give. One man took all of the meeting time of our group week after week trying to determine how committed everyone else was to a project that involved the purchase of a building. We could not get him off the subject. Then in a moment of enlightenment he was able to see that he did not know how he himself stood in relation to the project. He was determined to find out how responsible everyone else planned to be, since he was not to be counted on. The insight was liberating because he was able to switch his attention from his struggle with the commitments of others to a struggle with his own, which was more profitable to him and was fraught with less anxiety.

Whenever our participation in a group is dependent on another person's being there, or on what another person does, then we are in a real sense at that person's mercy. If my decision is dependent upon the commitment that someone else makes, I am in a vulnerable and precarious spot. I am unpredictable enough myself without having also to contend with the unpredictableness of another human being. If I come to my own free decision to participate in bringing a project into being, what others do, or fail to do, does not weigh as heavily with me. Their actions can mean failure or success for an undertaking, but they do not create division in me or make me the accuser of others. My life does not fall and rise on the moves that others make. When I have dealt with what I am willing to risk or sacrifice to make something possible, I am willing to leave the other person to struggle with these same questions and come in his own time to his decision.

In a class in Christian Community that my church offers we use role-playing to illustrate how mission groups are formed. Everyone knows that at the end of the two hour session the groups will dissolve. Because we are not "playing for keeps," there is a spontaneity among class members that is not as evident on other occasions when we talk about mission.

The class begins with ten minutes of silence during which time each one is to think about a mission that he would like to carry out. At the end of that time those who have thought of a project which excites them issue a call to members of the class. Those who are not ready to sound their own call are asked to listen to the calls of others to see whether they can respond to any one of them. A class of sixteen will usually form three or four mission groups. And each new group is given the assignment of identifying the gifts of its members: prior, spiritual director, shepherd, teacher, etc.; and then of deciding the strategy and disciplines essential for the accomplishment of the mission.

In this process we make all kinds of discoveries about ourselves. Some groups are so excited about their missions and their gifts that it is not at all unusual for them to continue to meet and explore mission. Frequently, people who have been around for years and have never felt pulled by anything are attracted by a number of possibilities. When what we say does not bind us to a long-term commitment and we are not under pressure to succeed or please others, we are free to experiment and explore outlandish possibilities. Eric Hoffer says that "We are more ready to try the untried when what we do is inconsequential. Hence the remarkable fact that many inventions had their birth as toys. In the Occident the first machines were mechanical toys, and such crucial instruments as the telescope and microscope were first conceived as playthings."

As the patron of gifts, the church must provide an abundance of unthreatening situations in which children from one to 101 have an opportunity to play and consider for themselves all manner of ridiculous and absurd adventures. When we are ready, however, to put aside our important play and take up the matter of exercising our gifts day by day in the solid reality of the world, another important aspect of the subject of gifts will loom for the creative person—the possibility of failure. As long as we are repeating ourselves, we have a certain confidence that what we have done once we can do again. But when we use our gifts to create something out of nothing, the element of risk is present. We can lose our time, our reputation, our money, even the friends who value us for our achievements.

I have always been impressed by the large number of plays that open and close on Broadway in the early months of their performance. The plays are chosen by people who have been in theater all their lives, have read hundreds of plays in preparation for choosing one, and have often produced countless others. With few exceptions all the persons involved in the production of a play—director, manager, actors, actresses, scene designer—are seasoned artists and the choice of the experts. Thousands of dollars are invested before the production ever opens, but no one can know in advance whether the exercising of all this talent will cohere in a creative act of the imagination, let alone become a play successful enough to run an entire season. Yet such highly visible failures in this and other areas do not help reduce the demand for achievement that ordinary people put on themselves and their friends.

When we do not allow ourselves the possibility of failure, the Spirit cannot work in us. We are controlled by perfectionistic strivings that inhibit the mysterious meshing of divergent lines within us. Spontaneity dies and the emergence of the unexpected ceases to be a possibility. We are literally tied and bound. In her book, *Centering*, Mary Caroline Richards writes that at one time she grieved because she could not make a close-fitting lid for a canister, a teapot, or a casserole. Then a friend, who was obviously a patron of gifts, sent her an ancient Korean pot, saying that he thought she would like it because it looked like something she might have made. She loved it at once. "Its lid didn't fit at all!" she writes, "Yet it was a museum piece, so to speak. Why, I mused, do I require of myself what I do not require of this pot? Its lid does not fit, but it inspires my spirit when I look at it and handle it. So I stopped worrying. Now I have very little trouble making lids that fit."[8]

In our culture we are so success-oriented that we have little understanding of the creative act. We want to know in advance that what we do will measure up and be judged acceptable. We applaud those who are successfully repeating themselves, while the innovative person is, at best, tolerated. Even if the creator should succeed, he is in difficulty because the new is threatening in that it differs from the norm.

We cannot exercise our gifts and at the same time be defenders of the status quo. Our gifts put us in tension with things as they are. Often the creator takes us where we do not want to go, trampling over our stereotypes in an effort to show us what we have not seen before. This is another reason why the creative person needs a patron saint who will not only comfort and protect him from envy, but will be around to encourage and support when the exercising of his gifts evokes fear in others.

Ultimately the fear of failure must be conquered in ourselves. I doubt that one ever wins this battle without having learned humility. We must be content to be who we are and not to put our sights so high that they do not correspond with our gifts. Also, while we listen soberly to our critics, we will do well to remember what William Blake told us—that we are not better for another man's praise or worse for his blame. This is hard for a creator to know, especially in the early stages of a work when there are no real lines of separation between who he is and what he has made. We cannot make something where nothing existed, whether it be a poem, a house, or a painting, without breathing life into it so that it may itself breathe—each is bone of our bone and flesh of our flesh. "Then the Lord God formed a man from the dust of the ground and breathed into his nostrils the breath of life. Thus the man became a living creature" (Gen. 2: 71 NEB). So it is with the continuing act of creation. "Creativeness in the world is, as it were, the eighth day of creation."[9]

In the beginning we must quietly hover over and protect the nascent or germinating thought until it has toughness and durability. New and emerging ideas that have not been nurtured in their own seedbed should not be spoken of at great length, if at all. They will not survive if they are exposed too early, partly because they are too vulnerable to resist attack or even questioning, and partly because words give them a form and launch them prematurely, taking from the creator the inner necessity to work with them and give them shape in stone or wood or deliberate words. If the creator does make the effort to write the story he has disclosed to another or paint the picture he has described, he has the feeling of repeating himself.

Unless we fall into sin and make idols of the work of our hands, in time a natural separation will take place between us and what we have wrought. When an idea or a piece of work is fully formed we will be able to send it into the world as the parent does a child. We may never respond indifferently to attacks upon it, but we will not feel that we ourselves are being attacked. We acquire a detachment which enables us to turn to the next idea that is hovering at the edges of sight waiting to claim us for the work of creation.

The phrase, "work of creation," raises a whole new subject that anyone seriously concerned with his gifts must consider. As we named gifts in our community we found that many of us were under the illusion that if a gift were really ours and we were engaged in doing what we were intended to do, no pain would be involved. As for any agony—this was certainly a sign that we had misheard directions. If some of us found ourselves laboring to accomplish a goal, or with large obstacles in our way, we were quite ready to conclude that we were obviously not called to work in this area and that we had better withdraw in favor of someone whose calling it was.

We look at a completed work—a painting, a piece of writing, a gourmet dinner— and we think that, like Minerva, it sprang full grown from the creator's head. At the very most, all that was required of him was a certain number of hours at the canvas, typewriter, or stove until the work emerged. I still remember an old cartoon showing a typewriter clicking away by itself while the author stood at the door calling to his wife, "Edna, come quick! I've got a book that's writing itself!" That fantasy about the creations of others is not at all uncommon. Such an illusion about the work of others makes us feel inferior. We want to take our little talent and bury it away. This attitude also contributes to the problems of those who toil to develop their gifts, for the rest of us make heavy demands on them. When we have not exercised our own capacity to create, we do not know what it is to wrestle with the angel, or we believe that once the blessing is given it lasts forever. When something needs to be done, we say, "So-and-so is good at that. Ask him to do it," not having the vaguest idea what we ask, or that we might do as well at a given task if we were to put in equal hours of labor.

The only purpose innocence can serve is to keep us from knowing the price of the "work of creation," but then neither do we know the joy. We never find fulfilled in ourselves the words, "Enter into the joy of the master." Having no investment of pain and labor, we have no return of self-worth and love.

If we are to be creators, we must begin to think in terms of a whole new work ethic. The reward will not be in higher wages, another rung on the ladder, the acclaim of our peers, but in creative forces which flow within us and accomplish in our own lives the gracious work of transformation. We exercise our own gifts and somewhere along the way we ourselves become patron saints of gifts.

Exercise I

This week the exercise is to become more aware of your special talents—the gifts through which your real self can be expressed, the gifts that will let you know what it is you are to do and become. Our talents are the conveyors of personality. They hold our reconciling acts. As we become aware of them and listen to their demand to be exercised, they enlarge the self and give depth and height to the inner world. If they are not used, they atrophy, and the self is diminished.

If you do not know what gifts are yours to exercise at this stage in your life, ask for the gift of the Holy Spirit, and practice for five minutes the withdrawing of your attention from all outward and inward considerations[1]. By will, concentrate your attention deep within yourself. When you have reached a place of quiet, begin to think about your gifts. Pay attention to the images that pass across your mind. Write them down and ponder their meaning. Fantasize what you would do if you could do anything in the world you chose. Watch yourself doing what you would most love to do and name the talents essential for that fantasy to become real. Then see whether you can discover those talents in yourself. What we would most love to do is a strong indication of what we have the potential to achieve.

When you have named your talents or gifts, list the risks that you will have to take in order to actualize them. What will you have to give up if you are to develop these gifts ? What are the obstacles that you foresee?

After you have given deep consideration to your own gifts, identify the gifts of each person in the group doing these exercises with you. A fun way of doing this is to ask each group member to put his or her name at the top of an 8 1/2 x 11 sheet of paper. Then have them list under their names three persons, living or dead, whom they admire and the gift that draws them to each person. When this has been done have members make a new heading entitled: MY GIFTS. Under this heading have them list the three gifts they have most admired in their heroes or heroines, and assure them that they would not have admired a gift they did not possess in a large degree themselves, even though it might be in a latent state.

The sheets should then be passed around the room, so that each person has an opportunity to add to each list what he or she sees as that person's gift. Members may then take turns reading aloud their lists of gifts. Each might be encouraged to stand and begin by saying, "My name is —— and my gifts are ——." This exercise is practice in identifying, owning and confirming gifts. The exercise can also be used in families. I once used it to everyone's enjoyment at a Christmas dinner party. Each of us has the power to evoke and confirm another's gift. This power may be the greatest gift any one of us can have.

Give attention to what will help or hinder you and group members in the actualization of your gifts.

Be sure to read each day one of the selections that follow. They give encouragement in the work of creating.

"For it will be as when a man going on a journey called his servants and entrusted to them his property; to one he gave five talents, to another two, to another one, to each according to his ability. Then he went away. He who had received the five talents went at once and traded with them; and he made five talents more. So too, he who had the two talents made two talents more. But he who had received the one talent went and dug in the ground and hid his master's money. Now after a long time the master of those servants came and settled accounts with them. And he who had received the five talents came forward, bringing five talents more, saying, 'Master, you delivered to me five talents; here I have made five talents more.' His master said to him, 'Well done, good and faithful servant, you have been faithful over a little, I will set you over much; enter into the joy of your master.'And he also who had the two talents came forward, saying, 'Master, you delivered to me two talents; here I have made two talents more.' His master said to him, 'Well done, good and faithful servant; you have been faithful over a little, I will set you over much; enter into the joy of your master.' He also who had received the one talent came forward, saying, 'Master, I knew you to be a hard man, reaping where you did not sow, and gathering where you did not winnow; so I was afraid, and I went and hid your talent in the ground. Here you have what is yours. 'But his master

answered him, 'You wicked and slothful servant! You knew that I reap where I have not sowed, and gather where I have not winnowed? Then you ought to have invested my money with the bankers, and at my coming I should have received what was my own with interest. So take the talent from him, and give it to him who has the ten talents. For to every one who has will more be given, and he will have abundance; but from him who has not, even what he has will be taken away. And cast the worthless servant into the outer darkness; there men will weep and gnash their teeth."
—Matthew 25:14-30 (RSV).

"The unfulfilled potential, the unlived experience, haunts consciousness, for deep down in every man lives the knowledge that the sin of unfulfillment is a sin against the Holy Ghost, the spirit of life whose breath is the Awakener. In Christ's parable unfulfillment is the sin of the slothful servant who, receiving the one talent from his master, wraps it "in a clean white napkin" and buries it until he is called upon for an accounting. He plays safe and so forfeits that which was originally given. Similarly in life one may hoard a chosen virtue, running no risk of losing it through living experience that may require encountering evil within oneself or risking its loss

in the market place of life. Too late, perhaps, we discover that what we have saved through false caution we have most truly lost. We may plead unconsciousness, yet, if we look back with honesty, we know that at a critical moment, an experience, or a dream, or a voice came to arouse a consciousness of new life which we refused. We must accept the unpleasant knowledge that in that moment we chose to remain unconscious, and that "before the bar of nature and fate unconsciousness is never accepted as an excuse; on the contrary, there are very severe penalties for it." (Jung, *Answer to Job.*)
—Frances G. Wickes, *The Inner World of Choice*, p. 53.

I can sit at my typewriter and imagine a time when man will be able to engineer planets in other solar systems into orbits suitable for the support of human life and "seed" them to produce an environment similar to our own. I can imagine art-works that feed the spectators, or a buffalo riding on the back of a giant sea turtle, or transmitting the genetic code of man to planets in outer space on electronic wave impulses. This fundamental *freedom* of the imagination places it beyond the control of even the most fanatical police state. Yet the tragedy is that we constantly destroy man's imagination by labeling it "day-dreaming," "unrealistic," "impractical." In our society, at the age of five, 90 percent of the population measures "high creativity." By the age of seven, the figure has dropped to 10 percent. And the percentage of adults with high creativity is only two percent! Our creativity is destroyed not through the use of outside force, but through criticism, innuendo, subtle psychological means which the "well-trained" child learns to use upon himself! Most of us are our own "brain police."

But if Freud was right that nothing is ever lost to the unconscious, then the creativity of early childhood must still be present in all of us—latent, repressed, crippled —but present! No less a man than William Blake, one of the great creative geniuses of all times, could say, "You have the same intuition as I, only you do not trust or cultivate it. You can *see* what I do, if you choose." One of the fundamental freedoms of a democracy should be the right of every individual to his own creative expressions.
—Finley Eversole, "The Politics of Creativity."

The following spring I was to leave the preparatory school and enter a university. I was still undecided, however, as to where and what I was to study. I had grown a thin mustache, I was a full-grown man, and yet I was completely helpless and without a goal in life. Only one thing was certain: the voice within me, the dream image. I felt the duty to follow this voice blindly wherever it might lead me. But it was difficult and each day I rebelled against it anew. Perhaps I was mad, as I thought at moments; perhaps I was not like other men? But I was able to do the same things the others did; with a little effort and industry I could read Plato, was able to solve problems in trigonometry or follow a chemical analysis. There was only one thing I could not do: wrest the dark secret goal from myself and keep it before me as others did who knew exactly what they wanted to be — professors, lawyers, doctors, artists, however long this would take them and whatever difficulties and advantages this decision would bear in its wake. This I could not do. Perhaps I would become something similar, but how was I to know? Perhaps I would have to continue my search for years on end and would not become anything, and would not reach a goal. Perhaps I would reach this goal but it would turn out to be an evil, dangerous, horrible one?

I wanted only to try to live in accord with the promptings which came from my true self. Why was that so very difficult?
—Hermann Hesse, *Demian*, p. 80.

The Ancients said, 'Know thyself,'and the moderns say, 'Be yourself.' It is not the same thing, but the recommendations do not conflict, and may even be necessary to each other's fulfillment. We are familiar with the advice to go ahead and be ourselves at all costs, and do what we genuinely want to do. That sounds good. But then, as a modern writer has pointed out, it is not always so easy to know what we do like, or like to do. That must depend on knowing what we really are, which again means taking trouble, and a period at any rate of uncertainty. That is never a comfortable period! It seems easier and safer to follow the crowd. So we choose the things that other people apparently find worth having, and try to persuade ourselves that we have chosen them freely. But then perhaps we discover that they are not 'our things' at all, and they bring us little satisfaction. Unless we first know ourselves, it seems improbable that we can carry out the rest of the programme. We may agree that we are not likely to make a success of trying to be something other than our true self. But what is this 'self' and how are we to know it?

–E. Graham Howe & L. Le Mesurier, *The Open Way*,p. 111.

I am a question-asker and a truth-seeker. I do not have much in the way of status in life, nor security. I have been on quest, as it were, from the beginning. For a long time I thought there was something wrong with me: no ambition, no interest in tenure, always on the march, changing every seven years, from landscape to landscape. Certain elements were constant: the poetry, the desire for relationship, the sense of voyage. But lately I have developed also a sense of destination, or destiny. And a sense that if I am to be on quest, I must expect to live like a pilgrim; I must keep to the inner path. I must be able to be whoever I am.

For example, it seemed strange to me, as to others, that, having taken my Ph.D. in English, I should then in the middle of my life, instead of taking up a college professorship, turn to the art of pottery. During one period, when people asked me what I did, I was uncertain what to answer; I guessed I could say I taught English, wrote poetry, and made pottery. What was my occupation? I finally gave up and said "Person."

—Mary Caroline Richards, *Centering in Pottery, Poetry, and the Person*, pp. 13-14.

You ask whether your verses are good. You ask me. You have asked others before. You send them to magazines. You compare them with other poems, and you are disturbed when certain editors reject your efforts. Now (since you have allowed me to advise you) I beg you to give up all that. You are looking outward, and that above all you should not do now. Nobody can counsel and help you, nobody. There is only one single way. Go into yourself. Search for the reason that bids you write; find out whether it is spreading out its roots in the deepest places of your heart, acknowledge to yourself whether you would have to die if it were denied you to write. This above all—ask yourself in the stillest hour of your night: *must I* write? Delve into yourself for a deep answer. And if this should be affirmative, if you may meet this earnest question with a strong and simple *"I must,"* then build your life according to this necessity; your life even into its most indifferent and slightest hour must be a sign of this urge and a testimony to it. Then draw near to Nature. Then try, like some first human being, to say what you see and experience and love and lose. Do not write love-poems; avoid at first those forms that are too facile and commonplace: they are the most difficult, for it takes a great, fully matured power to give something of your own where good and even excellent traditions come to mind in quantity. Therefore save yourself from these general themes and seek those which your own everyday life offers you; describe your sorrows and desires, passing thoughts and the belief in some sort of beauty—describe all these with loving, quiet, humble sincerity, and use, to express yourself, the things of your environment, the images from your dreams, and the objects of your memory. If your daily life seems poor, do not blame it; blame yourself, tell yourself that you are not poet enough to call forth its riches; for to the creator there is no poverty and no poor indifferent place. And even if you were in some prison the walls of which let none of the sounds of the world come to your senses — would you not then still have your childhood, that precious, kingly possession, that treasure-house of memories? Turn your attention thither. Try to raise the submerged sensations of that ample past; your personality will grow more firm, your solitude will widen and will become a dusky dwelling past which the noise of others goes by far away. — And if out of this turning inward, out of this absorption into your own world *verses* come, then it will not occur to you to ask anyone whether they are good *verses*. Nor will you try to interest magazines in your poems: for you will see in them your fond natural possession, a fragment and a voice of your life. A work of art is good if it has sprung from necessity. In this nature of its origin lies the judgment of it: there is no other. Therefore, my dear sir, I know no advice for you save this: to go into yourself and test the deeps in which your life takes rise; at its source you will find the answer to the question whether you *must* create. Accept it, just as it sounds, without inquiring into it. Perhaps it will turn out that you are called to be an artist. Then take that destiny upon yourself and bear it, its burden and its greatness, without ever asking what recompense might come from outside. For the creator must be a world for himself and find everything in himself and in Nature to whom he has attached himself.

But perhaps after this descent into yourself and into your inner solitude you will have to give up becoming a poet; (it is enough, as I have said, to feel that one could live without writing: then one must not attempt it at all). But even then this inward searching which I ask of you will not have been in vain. Your life will in any case find its own ways thence, and that they may be good, rich and wide I wish you more than I can say.

What more shall I say to you? Everything seems to me to have its just emphasis; and after all I do only want to advise you to keep growing quietly and seriously throughout your whole development; you cannot disturb it more rudely than by looking outward and expecting from outside replies to questions that only your inmost feeling in your most hushed hour can perhaps answer.
—Rainer Maria Rilke, *Letters to a Young Poet*, pp. 18-21.

We ask "how?" and we ask to be shown the means only because we are unwilling to give ourselves totally to the search for what is required. What does the Lord require of you? The prophet Micah has given a very famous answer to this question. But I should like to suggest another answer, namely, that what the Lord requires of you, what life requires of you, is that you should knock yourself out your whole life long to find out what is required of you. And until You do that, you are not really being honest to God, or to life. You're trying to get by with something less than what is really required, to come by reality at bargain basement prices. But reality is never on sale, its price is never marked down. We are required to sell all that we have in order to be able to pay for it.

St. Francis de Sales was once approached by a disciple who said to him, "Sir, you speak so much about the love of God, but you never tell us how to achieve it. Won't you tell me how one comes to love God?" And St. Francis replied, "There is only one way and that is to love Him." "But you don't quite understand my question. What I asked was, 'How do you engender this love of God?'" And St. Francis said, "By loving Him." Once again the pupil came back with the same question, "But what steps do you take? Just what do you do in order to come into the possession of this love?" And all St. Francis said was, "You begin by loving and you go on loving and loving teaches you how to love. And the more you love, the more you learn to love." And in our own day, Martin Buber has spoken in the same vein, replying to the question:

"What are we to do?" "What is to be done?" If you mean by this question, "What is *one* to do?" there is no answer. *One* is not to do anything. *One* cannot help himself. With *one*, there is nothing to begin. With *one*, it is all over. He who contents himself with explaining or asking what he is to do, talks and lives in a vacuum.

But he who poses the question with the earnestness of his soul on his lips and means, "What have I to do?" he is taken by the hand by comrades he does not know but whom he will soon become familiar with, and they answer, "You shall not withhold yourself."

Thus again, the Way will teach you the Way, and the Way is learning not to withhold yourself. The Way is learning to be with life, in life, one with life, more and more. And there is nothing else to be learned. And for this there are no techniques. We must not, therefore, look to a conference on religion and psychology to relieve us of the task of living our own lives. There are many who look to psychology or psychotherapy or to spiritual writing for answers, and this is all right up to a point, but pushed too far it becomes

an escape from oneself, from one's own reality. If you keep asking, "How shall I do it?" you are not meeting your own life situation. Only your own life can teach you how it is to be lived. If we turn to psychology or to religion because we are afraid to face our own life, to sweat and to toil and to shed tears and to learn to love in the context of our own existential situation, then psychology and religion become obstacles to reality. Since this is what happens to most people, it can perhaps be said paradoxically that the greatest obstacle to religion is religion, and the greatest obstacle to self- understanding is psychology. One must never approach these as forms of knowledge which will exempt one from the necessity of actually living and learning from life itself.
—Bernard Phillips, *The Search Will Make You Free*, pp. 30-31.

    This inner core, even though it is biologically based and "instinctoid," is weak in certain senses rather than strong. It is easily overcome, suppressed or repressed. It may even be killed off permanently. Humans no longer have instincts in the animal sense, powerful, unmistakable inner voices which tell them unequivocally what to do, when, where, how and with whom. All that we have left are instinct-remnants. And furthermore, these are weak, subtle and delicate, very easily drowned out by learning, by cultural expectations, by

fear, by disapproval, etc. They are *hard* to know, rather than easy. Authentic self-hood can be defined in part as being able to hear these impulse-voices within oneself, i.e., to know what one really wants or doesn't want, what one is fit for and what one is *not* fit for, etc. It appears that there are wide individual differences in the strength of these impulse-voices.
—Abraham H. Maslow, *Toward a Psychology of Being, p.191.*

You compel many to change their opinion about you; they hold that very much against you. You approached them and yet went on past them: that they will never forgive you.

You go above and beyond them: but the higher you climb, the smaller you appear to the eye of envy. And he who flies is hated most of all.
—Friedrich Nietzsche,*Thus Spoke Zarathustra*, p. 89.

Where there is a striving for power and domination, one can with certainty find the trait of envy in addition. The gulf between an individual and his supernaturally high goal expresses itself in the form of an inferiority complex. It oppresses him, and acquires such an influence upon his general behavior and his attitude toward life that one has the impression that he is a long way from his goal. His own low evaluation of himself, and his constant dissatisfaction with life are unfailing indicators thereof. He begins to spend his time in measuring the success of others, in occupying himself with what others think of him, or of what others have accomplished. He is always the victim of a sense of neglect, and he feels that discrimination has been exercised against him. Such an individual may actually have more than others. The various manifestations of this feeling of being neglected are indices of an unsatisfied vanity, of a desire to have more than one's neighbor, or indeed, to have everything. Envious people of this type do not say that they wish to have everything because the actual existence of a social feeling prevents them from thinking these thoughts. But they act *as if* they wanted to have everything.

The feeling of envy which grows up in the process of this constant measuring of others' success does not lead to greater possibilities of achieving happiness. The universality of the social feeling causes the universal dislike of envy; yet there are but few who are not capable of some envy. None of us is entirely free of it. In the even tenor of life it may often not be evident, yet when a man suffers, or feels himself oppressed, or lacks for money, food, dress, or warmth, when his hope for the future is darkened, and he sees

70

no way out of his unfortunate situation, then envy appears.

We human beings stand today in the beginning of our civilization. Although our ethics and our religion forbid feelings of envy, we have not yet psychologically matured enough to do without them. One can well understand the envy of the impecunious. Such envy would be incomprehensible only if someone could prove that, placed in the same position, he would not be envious. All that we wish to say concerning this is that we must reckon with this factor in the contemporary situation in the human soul. The fact is that envy arises in the individual, or in the group, as soon as one limits their activity too much. But when envy appears in those most disagreeable forms which we cannot ever approve, we do not actually know any means of obviating such envy and the frequently associated hate. One thing is clear to everyone who lives in our society, and that is that one should not put such tendencies to the test, nor provoke them; and that one should have sufficient tact not to accentuate any envious expressions which might be expected. Nothing is bettered by this course, it is true. Yet the very least we can demand of an individual is this: that he should not parade any temporary superiority over his fellows. He may too easily injure someone thereby.

The inseparable connection between the individual and society is indicated in the origin of this character trait. No one can lift himself above society, demonstrate his power over his fellows, without simultaneously arousing the opposition of others who want to prevent his success. Envy forces us to institute all those measures and rules whose purpose is the establishment of equality in all human beings. Finally we come rationally to a thesis which we have felt intuitively: *the law of the equality of all human beings.* This law may not be broken without immediately producing opposition and discord. It is one of the fundamental laws of human society.

The manifestations of envy are easily recognized, sometimes, indeed, in the very look of an individual. Envious traits which people have long used in their figures of speech have a physiological concomitant. One speaks of "green" or "pale" envy, pointing to the fact that envy influences the circulation of the blood. The organic expression of envy is found in the peripheral contraction of the capillary arteries.

So far as the pedagogic significance of envy is concerned, we have but one course. Since we cannot entirely destroy it, we must make it useful. This can be done by giving it a channel in which it can be made fruitful, without causing too great a shock to the psychic life. This holds good for the individual, as well as for the crowd. In the case of the individual we can prescribe an occupation which will elevate his self-esteem; in the life of nations, we can do nothing else than to show new ways to the development of innate, undeveloped powers to those nations which feel themselves neglected.

Anyone who has been envious all his life is useless for communal life. He will be interested solely in taking something away from another, in depriving him in some fashion, and in disturbing him. Simultaneously he will have the tendency to fix alibis for the goals which he has not attained, and blame others for his failures. He will be a fighter, a marplot, one who has no great love for good relationships, who has no part in the business of making himself useful to others. Since he hardly gives himself the trouble to sympathize with the situation of others, he has little understanding for human nature. He will not be moved by the fact that someone else suffers because of his actions. Envy may go so far as to lead a man to feel pleasure in the pain of his neighbor.
—Alfred Adler,*Understanding Human Nature*, pp. 178-80.

Then Herod summoned the wise men secretly and ascertained from them what time the star appeared; and he sent them to Bethlehem, saying, "Go and search diligently for the child, and when you have found him bring me word, that I too may come and worship him." When they had heard the king they went their way; and lo, the star which they had seen in the East went before them, till it came to rest over the place where the child was. When they saw the star, they rejoiced exceedingly with great joy; and going into the house they saw the child with Mary his mother, and they fell down and worshiped him. Then, opening their treasures, they offered him gifts, gold and frankincense and myrrh. And being warned in a dream not to return to Herod, they departed to their own country by another way.

—Matthew 2:7-12 (RSV).

Thought today of envy—the envy of Herod. It is a dread thought that another should take my place—another be considered greater than I. Kill off quickly the possibility of replacement. Secure my own position. Kill off Russia and China and keep America first. Kill the slumbering giant in every nation —

better still, kill the slumbering giant in every person.

As for the exercising of gifts, let everyone be cautious. The exercising of gifts evokes envy—makes enemies of those who, if you stay commonplace, would be your friends. Above all, do not exercise the gift of being yourself —this is the greatest threat of all. Kill off the woman who would be herself. Watch out, if you plan to be yourself. Such disturbance of the peace will not be allowed in many hearts.

Envy, the killer, strikes not only the head beneath the star, but the one who follows the star. Envy does not know that everyone has a star above his head. Small wonder that I dread my own envy, but then I also dread yours. I will protect us both and keep secret the fact that I am the possessor of gifts. And if you will be so kind, please do the same for me. Or is there another way— the way of the star? If in my envy, I will remember to look up, and search, and ask, will I find the star that leads to "the place of indescribable joy" (Matt. 2:10, Phillips), the place where one kneels down and worships? They say that from that place one rises up both a shepherd and a king—a servant and a leader. This is what the exercising of gifts is all about. It has to do with going to Bethlehem. But how many of us are wise?

—Elizabeth O'Connor, *A Meditation on the Christmas Story.*

Each one of us has some kind of vocation. We are all called by God to share in His life and in His Kingdom. Each one of us is called to a special place in the Kingdom. If we find that place we will be happy. If we do not find it, we can never be completely happy. For each one of us, there is only one thing necessary: to fulfill our own destiny, according to God's will, to be what God wants us to be.

We must not imagine that we only discover this destiny by a game of hide-and-seek with Divine Providence. Our vocation is not a sphinx's riddle, which we must solve in one guess or else perish. Some people find, in the end, that they have made many wrong guesses, and that their paradoxical vocation is to go through life guessing wrong. It takes them a long time to find out that they are happier that way.

In any case, our destiny is the work of two wills, not one. It is not an immutable fate, forced upon us without any choice of our own, by a divinity without heart.

Our vocation is not a supernatural lottery but the interaction of two freedoms, and, therefore, of two loves. It is hopeless to try to settle the problem of vocation outside the context of friendship and of love. We speak of Providence: that is a philosophical term. The Bible speaks of our Father in Heaven. Providence is, consequently, more than an institution, it is a person. More than a benevolent stranger, He is our Father. And even the term Father is too loose a metaphor to contain all the depths of the mystery: for He loves us more than we love ourselves, as if we were Himself. He loves us moreover with our own wills, with our own decisions. How can we understand the mystery of our union with God Who is closer to us than we are to ourselves? It is His very closeness that makes it difficult for us to think of Him. He Who is infinitely above us, infinitely different from ourselves, infinitely "other" from us, nevertheless dwells in our souls, watches over every movement of our life with as much love as if we were His own self. His love is at work bringing good out of all our mistakes and defeating even our sins.

In planning the course of our lives, we must remember the importance and the dignity of our own freedom. A man who fears to settle his future by a good act of his own free choice does not understand the love of God. For our freedom is a gift God has given us in order that He may be able to love us more perfectly, and be loved by us more perfectly in return.

—Thomas Merton, *No Man Is an Island*, pp. 107-8.

The parent who is interested in his child plays with him, works with him, spends time with him, leads him into various kinds of self-activity. In the words of Bietz, this parent paints talking pictures for his child — verbal pictures, orienting pictures, imaginative pictures, suggestive pictures, experimental pictures, molding and shaping pictures, both of the present and the future. He talks of what the child is, what he can be, and what he might become: "I can see that you're going to be able to get along with all kinds of people." He mentions possible goals and directions: "Can you imagine how it would be to fly an airplane? How would you like to be able to cure people who are sick? To make speeches in front of big audiences?" He is always ready to participate when the child wants to do a bit of day-dreaming because he respects the child for whatever he happens to be and whatever he may become. He has a sense of the endless possibilities open to the child, and tries to help him survey some of these possibilities. That is, he tries to help the child find himself, choose himself, create himself.

Unquestionably, psychic existence—a strong, clear feeling of personal identity—is the finest gift a parent can make to his child. It is the definitive parental gift, the gift which entitles one to call himself a parent. Helping his child toward personal identification is the area of real parental indispensability: others can wash diapers, teach arithmetic, and the like. Bringing children into physical existence is only the beginning of the basic parental responsibility. The real job is to bring them into psychic existence and to help them as far as possible along its distant reaches.

—Raymond Rogers, *Coming into Existence: The Struggle to Become an Individual, pp. 9-10.*

      A man, in order to make his place in the modern world, will push forward every element in his character that will help him rise to his desired goal. In order to do this, he has to neglect certain other aspects or values in his life. Let us say there is a bit of an artist, a poet, or a musician in him. In order to make his way in business, he pushes this inclination aside, thinking it just does not belong with his profession. Yet this gift was placed there by One other than himself, and he will not let it be neglected. Either the man comes back and picks up his interest in this field, or he dies spiritually and emotionally. The heart must have its nurture as well as the mind; the soul must be clothed as well as the body. It is no accident that Winston Churchill and President Eisenhower painted, or that President Truman played the piano, and Albert Schweitzer continued playing the organ.

—Charles B. Hanna, *The Face of the Deep*, p. 98.

A gift of any kind is a considerable responsibility. It is a mystery in itself, something gratuitous and wholly undeserved, something whose real uses will probably always be hidden from us. Usually the artist has to suffer certain deprivations in order to use his gift with integrity. Art is a virtue of the practical intellect, and the practice of any virtue demands a certain asceticism and a very definite leaving-behind of the niggardly part of the ego. The writer has to judge himself with a stranger's eye and a stranger's severity. The prophet in him has to see the freak. No art is sunk in the self, but rather, in art the self becomes self-forgetful in order to meet the demands of the thing seen and the thing being made.

.   .   .   .   .

If a writer is any good, what he makes will have its source in a realm much larger than that which his conscious mind can encompass and will always be a greater surprise to him than it can ever be to his reader.

Flannery O'Connor, *Mystery and Manners*, pp.81-82, 83.

I heard them talking to one another in murmurs and whispers. They talked about illness, money, shabby domestic cares. Their talk painted the walls of the dismal prison in which these men had locked themselves up. And suddenly I had a vision of the face of destiny.

Old bureaucrat, my comrade, it is not you who are to blame. No one ever helped you to escape. You, like a termite, built your peace by blocking up with cement every chink and cranny through which the light might pierce. You rolled yourself up into a ball in your genteel security, in routine, in the stifling conventions of provincial life, raising a modest rampart against the winds and the tides and the stars. You have chosen not to be perturbed by great problems, having trouble enough to forget your own fate as man. You are not the dweller upon an errant planet and do not ask yourself questions to which there are no answers. You are a petty bourgeois of Toulouse. Nobody grasped you by the shoulder while there was still time. Now the clay of which you were shaped has dried and hardened, and naught in you will ever awaken the sleeping musician, the poet, the astronomer that possibly inhabited you in the beginning.

—Antoine de Saint-Exupéry, *Wind, Sand and Stars*, p. 23.

The new gullibility of our particular time is not that of the man who believes too much, but that of the man who believes too little-the man who has lost his sense of the miracle-the man capable of believing that Creation is in some way an automatic or commonplace thing, or even that man himself, physically and psychically, can be dissected into neat packages susceptible to complete explanation.

When awe and wonder depart from our awareness, depression sets in, and after its blanket has lain smotheringly upon us for a while, despair may ensue, or the quest for kicks begin. The loss of wonder, of awe, of the sense of the sublime, is a condition leading to the death of the soul. There is no more withering state than that which takes all things for granted, whether with respect to human beings or the rest of the natural order. The blasé attitude means spiritual, emotional, intellectual, and creative death.

—Edmund Fuller, *Man in Modern Fiction*, pp. 163-64.

But each of us has been given his gift, his due portion of Christ's bounty. Therefore Scripture says:
'He ascended into the heights
with captives in his train;
he gave gifts to men.'
—Ephesians 4:7–8 (N.B).

82

Exercise II

In the last exercise your attention was focused primarily on the identification of your gifts. Now you are to think of a work that you would like to do. So often it is our call or a work which determines the gifts we will fully exercise. A work, if it is to create our lives and heal and restore the world, must be connected to our innermost self. It may be enrolling in an art class so that all those images that rise unpredictably in you may be given form, or it may be the founding of a soup kitchen or an institution, or writing a poem, or having a dinner party that will feed the hunger for community of those around your table.

Choose a work to do by listening to yourself—the still small voice within that speaks to you in images, wishes, dreams and fantasies, your own words and the words of others.

If you make a mistake and choose the wrong task, you will have learned something about yourself and can take courage and choose again. This is a good time to practice moving ahead in the face of any fears you might have. You will find those fears fading away as you begin to act. If you have no feelings of uncertainty, it is not likely that you are doing much adventuring into the new for the unknown always stirs in us some anxiety—waves of self-doubt. If we think we are alone in that response, we can know that we are caught by another illusion. When God told Moses that he was to deliver his people out of the hand of the Egyptians, Moses replied, "Who am I that I should go?" He raised question after question as to whether he was the one to accomplish the mission. Finally he said, "Oh, my Lord, I am not eloquent, either heretofore or since thou hast spoken to thy servant; but I am slow of speech and of tongue" (Exod. 4:10, RSV). Jeremiah had as difficult a time with his commissioning, "Ah, Lord God! Behold, I do not know how to speak, for I am only a youth!' (Jer. 1: 6, RSV).

Move into the silence within and listen to what God is saying to you. If you feel that he has overestimated your gifts, follow in the tradition of Moses and Jeremiah and tell him your fears. Then listen in quiet for his answer. As you practice this assignment you may want to picture Jesus standing there before you. Write in your journal the conversation that you have with him either as it is taking place or later as you reflect on it.

If out of your meditation comes an idea, a thought, a piece of work that you are to do, then carry it around with you, reflect on it, brood over it, ask what it wants, what it requires of you. Perhaps you will have the experience of all the world talking to you about your idea. An item in a newspaper, a meeting with a friend, a chance remark—each has the possibility of nourishing the mysterious spark of life that is growing in you. For everyone the experience is different, but it is not uncommon for an idea to expand in unforeseen ways. At first we must make a strenuous effort to stay with a work which is new and unformed, but as we give it any attention it takes shape and grows strong; then it will not let us go until it has its own place in the world. Here again our uncertainty enters the picture because we are never quite sure that we can bring into being the image that is secreted away in us. If we begin to wonder how others will respond to our offering, whether what we have to share will be pleasing to them, we run away from ourselves and are in immediate trouble. As Brother Lawrence picked up a piece of straw for the love of God, so we must take up our work for love of the Holy Spirit working in our lives.

Remember, also, that
the guides of the saints are punctuated with the
words toil, labor, work, strive. If we are to move
toward any immediate or distant goal, these words
will also describe our days. The writer of
Corinthians in listing the gifts said, "Leaders, exert
yourselves to lead." He might have said: "Prophets,
exert yourselves to prophesy; teachers, exert yourselves to teach..." As in contemplative prayer, so in
the work of co-creation, we toil and toil and then
one day the cloud begins to part, pieces fit together,
ideas and thoughts pour in from another realm and
we know that the work of creation has been going
on at two levels in us. Finally we have a piece of
sculpture, a story, a building that has something
more in it than all the conscious labor of our days.
Of a work like this we say that it is inspired. But,
of course, there are not many inspired pieces in the
world for not many of us are contemplatives.

Always before begin-
ning a piece of work, as before prayer, ask for the
gift of the Holy Spirit, and then practice the exercise of recollection so that your attention is
gathered in as you have learned to do. Meditate for
a long time on the work at hand, holding it quietly
before you and letting your spirit merge with it.
And then, before beginning your work, center your
attention once again deep in yourself so that what
emerges flows from the core of your being, and not
from some peripheral point on the circumference of

your life where all kinds of distractions and the opinions of others flow in and take you further from yourself. When you are centered deep in yourself, using your trained powers of concentration, give yourself to the work at hand, exercising the gifts that will give that work breath.

Though I wrote this having in mind a creative act of the imagination—making something out of nothing—the same meditative, contemplative attitude can be brought to ordinary tasks, the conferences we attend, the people that we meet.

If you do not immediately discover a special project to work on, while you wait for it to be given to you, practice each day doing one task with a contemplative attitude. In time you will see with new eyes and hear with new ears, and be better able to envision the path you are to follow.

After I had written this book I told several friends. Their response was polite and mild. Later I was able to tell them the book was going to be published. Almost to a man they used the words "I am proud of you." Proud of the results but not of the action.

Everyone but *me* looks back on my behavior in judgement. They can only see my acts coupled with their results. But I act *now*. And I cannot know the results. I give my actions their only possible meaning for me, and this meaning always issues from: "I am responding to this part of me and not to that part."

I don't live in a laboratory: I have no way of knowing what results my actions will have. To live my life for results would be to sentence myself to continuous frustration and to hang over my head the threat that death may at any moment make my having lived a waste. My only sure reward is *in* my actions and not from them. The quality of my reward is in the depth of my response, the centralness of the part of me I act from.

Because the results are unpredictable, no effort of mine is doomed to failure. And even a failure will not take the form I imagine. The most realistic attitude for me to have toward future consequences is "it will be interesting to see what happens."

Excitement, dejection and boredom assume a knowledge of results that I cannot have.
—Hugh Prather, *Notes to Myself.*

A woman traveling in India chanced upon a maker of brass bowls. She picked up one of intricate design and asked its price. "Two annas." She thought of a friend who ran a "gifte shoppe" in America and of the profit she could make. "Ask him," she said to the interpreter, "how much they will be if I take fifty like this." The maker pondered. "Four annas." "But," said the bewildered woman, "tell him if I take so many they must be less, not more." The craftsman answered, "Tell the lady that if I repeat myself so many times I must have much money, for I shall need to go away into solitude so that my spirit can re-create itself."

I once found in a junk shop a Ming temple painting. The spirit of beauty shone through its battered surface. I took it home and sent for an Oriental man who restored such treasures. He stood before it a long time. "Yes, I will fix it. I will take it now." "What will it cost?" "I do not know." "When can you do it?" "I do not know." After several months he brought it back. He had re-created it. I stood reverently before it, then said, "No wonder it took so long." "Not the work," he answered. "That was swift; but the vision. I go into the country. I sit all day under a tree. It does not appear inside me. I am too far away. I may go again and again. One day I see it. Then I work quickly."

"And the price?" "Fifteen dollars." "For this!" "A man came yesterday bringing a terrible untrue object—such dreadful shape, such angry color—I charged him four hundred dollars, so now I charge you fifteen. It likes this room."

—Frances G. Wickes, *The Inner World of Choice*, pp.64-65.

And, if I may say it in a very condensed way, it is precisely the god-like in ourselves that we are ambivalent about, fascinated by and fearful of, motivated to and defensive against. This is one aspect of the basic human predicament, that we are simultaneously worms and gods ... Every one of our great creators, our god-like people, has testified to the element of courage that is needed in the lonely moment of creation, affirming something new (contradictory to the old). This is a kind of daring, a going out in front all alone, a defiance, a challenge. The moment of fright is quite understandable but must nevertheless be overcome if creation is to be possible. Thus to discover in oneself a great talent can certainly bring exhilaration but it also brings a fear of the dangers and responsibilities and duties of being a leader and of being all alone. Responsibility can be seen as a heavy burden and evaded as long as possible. Think of the mixture of feelings, of awe, humility, even of fright that have been reported to us, let us say, by people who have been elected President.

·   ·   ·   ·   ·

To make growth and self-actualization possible, it is necessary to understand that capacities, organs and organ systems press to function and express themselves and to be used and exercised, and that such use is satisfying, and disuse irritating. The muscular person likes to use his muscles, indeed, *has* to use them in order to "feel good" and to achieve the subjective feeling of harmonious, successful, uninhibited functioning (spontaneity) which is so important an aspect of good growth and psychological health. So also for intelligence, for the uterus, the eyes, the capacity to love. Capacities clamor to be used, and cease their clamor only when they *are* well used. That is, capacities are also needs. Not only is it fun to use our capacities, but it is also necessary for growth. The unused skill or capacity or organ can become a disease center or else atrophy or disappear, thus diminishing the person.

•   •   •   •   •

Growth has not only rewards and pleasures but also many intrinsic pains and always will have. Each step forward is a step into the unfamiliar and is possibly dangerous. It also means giving up something familiar and good and satisfying. It frequently means a parting and a separation, even a kind of death prior to rebirth, with consequent nostalgia, fear, loneliness and mourning. It also often means giving up a simpler and easier and less effortful life, in exchange for a more demanding, more responsible, more difficult life. Growth forward *is in spite* of these losses and therefore requires courage, will, choice, and strength in the individual, as well as protection, permission and encouragement from the environment, especially for the child.

—Abraham H. Maslow, *Toward A Psychology of Being*, pp. 61-62, 201, 204.

My own exploration of a psychology of hope will focus principally on the firm and constant relationship between hope and wishing. I assume that wishing and wanting reality in any or all its forms is basic to hope, and that it is hard to think of anything more in need of emphasis and analysis among us. For many are inclined toward apathy, which is to have no wishes; or toward not knowing what their real wishes are, which is to be separated from oneself; or toward throwing the interior gift of wishing and hoping out into the atmosphere, which is to let others do the wishing for us. How many can answer the questions: what do I wish? what do I want now?

These are the three evils we can come up against so far as a life of wishing and hoping is concerned: either we do not wish at all, or we have wishes and do not even know what they are, or we let others do the wishing and hoping for us. Any or all of these conditions can move us toward hopelessness, since any or all of them strike at the heart of our humanity and identity.

—William F. Lynch, *Images of Hope*, p. 110.

The very qualities which make us what we are constitute our special approach to God and our potential use for Him. Each man is created for the fulfillment of a unique purpose. His foremost task, therefore 'is the actualization of his unique, unprecedented and

never-recurring potentialities, and not the rep-
etition of something that another, and be it
even the greatest, has already achieved.' We
can revere the service of others and learn from
it, but we cannot imitate it. Neither ought
we envy another's particularity and place nor
attempt to impose our own particular way on
him. The way by which a man can reach God
is revealed to him only through the knowledge of his essential quality and inclination.
Man discovers this essential quality through
perceiving his 'central wish,' the strongest feeling
which stirs his inmost being. In many cases
he knows this central wish only in the form
of the particular passion which seeks to lead
him astray. To preserve and direct this passion he must divert it from the casual to the
essential, from the relative to the absolute.
He must prevent it from rushing at the objects which lie across his path, yet he must
not turn away from these objects but establish genuine relationship with them. 'Man's
task, therefore, is not to extirpate the evil urge,
but to reunite it with the good.' If man lends
his will to the direction of his passions, he
begins the movement of holiness which God
completes. In the hallowing which results,
'the total man is accepted, confirmed, and fulfilled.
This is the true integration of man.'
                    —Maurice S. Friedman, *Martin Buber, The*
                    Life of Dialogue, pp. 134-35.

WALLS

Without consideration, without pity, without shame
    they have built big and high walls around me.

And now I sit here despairing.
I think of nothing else: this fate gnaws at my mind;

for I had many things to do outside.
Ah why didn't I observe them when they were building
the walls?

But I never heard the noise or the sound of the builders.
Imperceptibly they shut me out of the world.
    —Constantine P. Cavafy, *The Complete Poems of Cavafy.*

    When you feel very strongly
about something, do you consider it difficult to put it into action? When you are
keen to play cricket, you play it with your
whole being, don't you? And do you call it
difficult? It is only when you don't vitally
feel the truth of something that you say it
is difficult to put it into action. You don't
love it. That which you love you do with
ardour, there is joy in it, and then what
society or what your parents may say does
not matter. But if you are not deeply con-
vinced, if you do not feel free and happy
in doing what you think is right, surely

your interest in it is false, unreal; therefore it becomes mountainous and you say it is difficult to put it into action.

In doing what you love to do there will of course be difficulties, but that won't matter to you, it is part of life. You see, we have made a philosophy of difficulty, we consider it a virtue to make effort, to struggle, to oppose.

I am not talking of proficiency through effort and struggle, but of the love of doing something. But don't battle against society, don't tackle dead tradition, unless you have this love in you, for your struggle will be meaningless and you will merely create more mischief. Whereas, if you deeply feel what is right and can therefore stand alone, then your action born of love will have extraordinary significance, it will have vitality, beauty.

•　　•　　•　　•　　•

Creativeness is not merely a matter of painting pictures or writing poems, which is good to do, but which is very little in itself. What is important is to be wholly discontented, for such total discontent is the beginning of the initiative which becomes creative as it matures; and that is the only way to find out what is truth, what is God, because the creative state is God.

So one must have this total discontent— but with joy. Do you understand?

One must be wholly discontented, not complainingly, but with joy, with gaiety, with love. Most people who are discontented are terrible bores; they are always complaining that something or other is not right, or wishing they were in a better position, or wanting circumstances to be different, because their discontent is very superficial. And those who are not discontented at all are already dead.

If you can be in revolt while you are young, and as you grow older keep your discontent alive with the vitality of joy and great affection, then that flame of discontent will have an extraordinary significance because it will build, it will create, it will bring new things into being. For this you must have the right kind of education, which is not the kind that merely prepares you to get a job or to climb the ladder of success, but the education that helps you to think and gives you space—space, not in the form of a larger bedroom or a higher roof, but space for your mind to grow so that it is not bound by any belief, by any fear.

• • • • •

To be inwardly rich is much more arduous than to be outwardly rich and famous; it needs much more care, much closer attention. If you have a little talent and know how to exploit it, you become famous; but inward richness does not come about in that way. To be inwardly rich the mind has to understand and put away the things that are not important, like wanting to be famous. Inward richness implies standing alone; but the man who wants to be famous is afraid to stand alone because he depends on people's flattery and good opinion.

•   •   •   •   •

Can you and I, who are simple, ordinary people, live creatively in this world without the drive of ambition which shows itself in various ways as the desire for power, position? You will find the right answer when you love what you are doing. If you are an engineer merely because you must earn a livelihood, or because your father or society expects it of you, that is another form of compulsion; and compulsion in any form creates a contradiction, conflict. Whereas, if you really love to be an engineer, or a scientist, or if you can plant a tree, or paint a picture, or write a poem, not to gain recognition but just because you love to do it, then you will find that you never compete with another. I think this is the real key: to love what you do.

But when you are young it is often very difficult to know what you love to do, because you want to do so many things. You want to be an engineer, a locomotive driver, an airplane pilot zooming along in the blue skies; or perhaps you want to be a famous orator or politician. You may want to be an artist, a chemist, a poet or a carpenter. You may want to work with your head, or do something with your hands. Is any of these things what you really love to do, or is your interest in them merely a reaction to social pressures? How can you find out? And is not the true purpose of education to *help* you to find out, so that as you grow up you can begin to give your whole mind, heart and body to that which you really love to do?

To find out what you love to do demands a great deal of intelligence; because, if you are afraid of not being able to earn a livelihood, or of not fitting into this rotten society, then you will never find out. But, if you are not frightened, if you refuse to be pushed into the groove of tradition by your parents, by your teachers, by the superficial demands of society, then there is a possibility of discovering what it is you really love to do. So, to discover, there must be no fear of not surviving.

But most of us are afraid of not surviving, we say, "What will happen to me if I don't do as my parents say, if I don't fit into this society?" Being frightened, we do as we are told, and in that there is no love, there is only contradiction; and this inner contradiction is one of the factors that bring about destructive ambition.

J. Krishnamurti, *Think on These Things* pp. 155, 40, 47, 52-53.

No matter how much we love a person, accept him, give him support, have warmth and affection for him, no matter how much we help him in so many ways, unless we can actually call him forth so that he is himself exercising the uniqueness God gave him, then the love is incomplete; he is not free, he is less than fully human.

We have said that the most effective thing we can do to call forth the gift of another is to employ our own gift in freedom. This may seem selfish at first. Aren't we supposed to help the other person? What does our own gift have to do with it? We start there.

The charismatic person is one who, by her very being, will be God's instrument in calling forth gifts. The person who is having the time of her life doing what she is doing has a way of calling forth the deeps of another. Such a person is herself Good News. She is the embodiment of the freedom of the new humanity. Verbal proclamation of the Good News becomes believable. The person who exercises her own gift in freedom can allow the Holy Spirit to do in others what He wants to do.

—Gordon Cosby, "The Calling Forth of the Charisma," (a sermon).

What is it about us, the public, and what is it about conformity itself that causes us all to require it of our neighbors and of our artists and then, with consummate fickleness, to forget those who fall into line and eternally celebrate those who do not?

Might not one surmise that there is some degree of nonconformity in us all, perhaps conquered or suppressed in the interest of our general well-being, but able to be touched or rekindled or inspired by just the quality of unorthodoxy which is so deeply embedded in art?

I doubt that good psychological or sociological opinion would allow such a view. On the contrary, I think that the most advanced opinion in these fields holds that we are by our natures doomed to conformity. We seem to be hemmed in by peer groups, hedged by tradition, struck dumb by archetypes; to be other-directed, inner-directed, outer-directed, over-directed. We are the organization man. It is not allowed that we may think for ourselves or be different or create something better than that which was before.

Since I do not myself aspire to being a sociologist, I do not feel particularly committed to correct sociological behavior. I don't care a rap about my peer group. And as for my tradition, brave though it may be and nostalgic, still I feel that I am on the whole well out of it. I cannot believe in Statistical

Man or Reisman Man (Reis-Man?) and I can even dream of a day when perhaps both shall be ranged alongside Piltdown Man in some wonderful museum of scientific follies.

Nonconformity is not only a desirable thing, it is a factual thing. One need only remark that all art is based upon nonconformity—a point that I shall undertake to establish-and that every great historical change has been based upon nonconformity, has been bought either with the blood or with the reputation of nonconformists. Without nonconformity we would have no Bill of Rights or Magna Charta, no public education system, no nation upon this continent, no continent, no science at all, no philosophy, and considerably fewer religions. All that is pretty obvious.

But it seems to be less obvious somehow that to create anything at all in any field, and especially anything of outstanding worth, requires nonconformity, or a want of satisfaction with things as they are. The creative person—the nonconformist—may be in profound disagreement with the present way of things, or he may simply wish to add his views, to render a personal account of matters.

•　　　•　　　•　　　•　　　•

Nonconformity is the basic pre-condition of art, as it is the pre-condition of good thinking and therefore of growth and

greatness in a people. The degree of nonconformity present—and tolerated—in a society
might be looked upon as a symptom of its state
of health.

•   •   •   •   •

The Education of an Artist

My capsule recommendation
for a course of education is as follows:
Attend a university if you possibly can. There is no content of knowledge
that is not pertinent to the work you will want
to do. But before you attend a university, work
at something for a while. Do anything. Get a
job in a potato field; or work as a grease mon-
key in an auto repair shop. But if you do work
in a field, do not fail to observe the look and
the feel of earth and of all things that you
handle— yes, even potatoes! Or, in the auto
shop, the smell of oil and grease and burning
rubber. Paint of course, but if you have to
lay aside painting for a time, continue to draw.
Listen well to all conversations and be instructed
by them and take all seriousness seriously.
Never look down upon anything or anyone
as not worthy of notice. In college or out of
college, read. And form opinions! Read Sophocles
and Euripides and Dante and Proust. Read
everything that you can find about art except
the reviews. Read the Bible; read Hume; read
Pogo. Read all kinds of poetry and know many

103

poets and many artists. Go to an art school, or two, or three, or take art courses at night if necessary. And paint and paint and draw and draw. Know all that you can, both curricular and noncurricular—mathematics and physics and economics, logic, and particularly history. Know at least two languages besides your own, but anyway, know French. Look at pictures and more pictures. Look at every kind of visual symbol, every kind of emblem; do not spurn sign-boards or furniture drawings or this style of art or that style of art. Do not be afraid to like paintings honestly or to dislike them honestly, but if you do dislike them retain an open mind. Do not dismiss any school of art, not the Pre-Raphaelites nor the Hudson River School nor the German Genre painters. Talk and talk and sit at cafes, and listen to everything, to Brahms, to Brubeck, to the Italian hour on the radio. Listen to preachers in small town churches and in big city churches. Listen to politicians in New England town meetings and to rabble-rousers in Alabama. Even draw them. And remember that you are trying to learn to think what you want to think, that you are trying to coordinate mind and hand and eye. Go to all sorts of museums and galleries and to the studios of artists. Go to Paris and Madrid and Rome and Ravenna and Padua. Stand alone in Sainte Chapelle, in the Sistine Chapel, in the Church of the Carmine in Florence. Draw and draw and paint and learn to work in many media;

try lithography and aquatint and silk-screen. Know all that you can about art, and by all means have opinions. Never be afraid to become embroiled in art or life or politics; never be afraid to learn to draw or paint better than you already do; and never be afraid to undertake any kind of art at all, however exalted to however common, but do it with distinction.

Anyone may observe that such an art education has no beginning and no end and that almost any other comparable set of experiences might be substituted for those mentioned, without loss. Such an education has, however, a certain structure which is dictated by the special needs of art.

—Ben Shahn, *The Shape of Content*, pp. 75-77, 87.

When Two Sing

When a man is singing and cannot lift his voice, and another comes and sings with him, another who can lift his voice, the first will be able to lift his voice too. That is the secret of the bond between spirits.

• • • • •

Pregnancy

When a man grows aware of a new way in which to serve God, he should carry it around with him secretly, and without uttering it, for nine months, as though he were pregnant with it, and let others know of it only at the end of that time, as though it were a birth.

—Martin Buber, *Ten Rungs: Hasidic Sayings*, pp. 84, 74.

Creativeness sometimes needs the protection of darkness, of being ignored. That is very obvious in the natural tendency many artists and writers have not to show their paintings or writings before they are finished. Until then they cannot stand even positive reactions. The passionate reactions of people to a painting, the exclamation, "Oh, this is wonderful!", may, even if meant in a positive way, entirely destroy the chiaroscuro, the mystical hidden weaving of fantasy which the artist needs. Only when he has finished his product can he expose it to the light of consciousness, and to the emotional reactions of others. Thus if you notice an unconscious fantasy coming up within you, you would be wise not to interpret it at once. Do not say that you know what it is and force it into consciousness. Just let it live with you, leaving it in the half-dark, carry it with you and watch where it is going or what it is driving at. Much later you will look back and wonder what you were doing all that time, that you were nursing a strange fantasy which then led to some unexpected goal. For instance, if you do some painting and have the idea that you could add this and that, then don't think, "I know what that means!" If you do, then push the thought away and just give yourself to it more and more so that the whole web of symbols expands in all its ramifications before you jump at its essential meaning.

—Marie-Louise von Franz, *Interpretation of Fairytales*, ch. 6 p. 12.

I learned this, at least, by my experiment: that if one advances confidently in the direction of his dreams, and endeavors to live the life which he has imagined, he will meet with a success unexpected in common hours. He will put some things behind, will pass an invisible boundary; new, universal, and more liberal laws will begin to establish themselves around and within him; or the old laws be expanded, and interpreted in his favor in a more liberal sense, and he will live with the license of a higher order of beings. In proportion as he simplifies his life, the laws of the universe will appear less complex, and solitude will not be solitude, nor poverty poverty, nor weakness weakness. If you have built castles in the air, your work need not be lost; that is where they should be. Now put the foundations under them.

—Henry David Thoreau, *Walden*, p. 215.

Good and evil, then, cannot be a pair of opposites like right and left or above and beneath. "Good" is the movement in the direction of home, "evil" is the aimless whirl of human potentialities without which nothing can be achieved and by which, if they take no direction but remain trapped in themselves, everything goes awry.

—Martin Buber, *Between Man and Man*, p. 78.

Each one who knows himself, for example, as called to a work which he has not done, each one who has not fulfilled a task which he knows to be his own, each who did not remain faithful to his vocation which he had become certain of—each such person knows what it means to say that "his conscience smites him."

—Martin Buber, *Eclipse of God,* p. 87.

Like clouds and wind that bring
no rain is the man who boasts of gifts he never
gives.

—Proverbs 25:14 (NEB).

But if you have nothing at all
to create, then perhaps you create yourself.

—C. G. Jung, *Collected Works*, 11 557.

We must learn neither to seek
nor to take our own advantage in any matter, but always to find and procure the advantage of God. For God does not give gifts,
nor did he ever give one, so that man might
keep it and take satisfaction in it; but all were
given — all he ever gave on earth or in heaven
— that he might give this one more: himself.
With all his giving, he is trying only to pre-
pare us for the gift that he himself is; and all
his works—all that he ever did on earth or in
heaven—he did for the sake of this one more:
to perfect our happiness. Therefore I say that
we must learn to look through every gift and
every event to God and never be content with
the thing itself. There is no stopping place in

this life -- no, nor was there ever one for any man, no matter how far along his way he'd gone. This above all, then, be ready at all times times for the gifts of God and always for new ones.

—Meister Eckhart, *Meister Eckhart, A Modern Translation, p. 32.*

NOTES

PREFACE

1. Elizabeth O'Connor, *Our Many Selves* (New York: Harper & Row, 1971).
2. ——, *Search for Silence* (Waco, Texas: Word Books, 1972).

GIFTS AND CREATIVITY

1. Calvin Tomkins, *Eric Hoffer, An American Odyssey* (New York: E. P. Dutton & Co., 1968), pp. 9-10.
2. The formation of mission groups is explained in detail in Elizabeth O'Connor, *Journey Inward, Journey Outward* (New York: Harper & Row, 1968).
3. Dietrich Bonhoeffer, *Life Together* (New York: Harper & Row, 1954), p. 94.
4. Minister, The Church of The Saviour, Washington, D.C.
5. Leslie H. Farber, *The Ways of the Will* (New York: Harper & Row, 1966), P. 130.
6. William F. Lynch, *Images of Hope* (New York: New American Library, Mentor Books, 1965), p. 189.
7. From *Psychology Today*, March 1968.
8. Mary Caroline Richards, *Centering in Pottery, Poetry, and the Person* (Middletown, Conn.: Wesleyan University Press, 1964), p. 23.
9. Nicolas Berdyaev, The Divine and the Human (London: Bles, 1949), ch. 13

.EXERCISE I

1. In the literature of prayer this is called "recollection" or being present to one's deeper self. A full explanation and exercises in recollection and meditation are given in a companion volume to this book, Elizabeth O'Connor, *Search for Silence* (San Diego, CA., LuraMedia,1986).

BIBLIOGRAPHY

BOOKS

Adler, Alfred. *Understanding Human Nature.* Translated by W. Biran
    Wolfe. Greenwich, Conn.: Fawcett World, 1968. (Hardbound ed.,
    New York: Humanities Press, 1928.)

Berdyaev, Nicolas. *The Divine and the Human.* London: Bles, 1949.

Bonhoeffer, Dietrich. *Life Together.* Translated by J. W. Doberstein.
    New York: Harper & Row, 1954.

Buber, Martin. *Between Man and Man.* Boston: Beacon Press,
    1955. New York: Macmillan, 1965.

—— *Eclipse of God.* New York: Harper & Bros., 1952.

—— *Ten Rungs: Hasidic Sayings.* New York: Schocken
    Books, 1947.

Cavafy, Constantine P. *Complete Poems of Cavafy:* New York: Harcourt,
    Brace & World, 1961.

Eckhart, Meister. *Meister Eckhart, a Modern Translation.* Translated by
    Raymond B. Blakney. New York: Harper & Row, 1941.

Farber, Leslie H. *The Ways of the Will.* New York: Harper & Row, 1966.

Friedman, Maurice S., *Martin Buber, The Life of Dialogue.* Chicago:
    University of Chicago Press, 1955.

Fuller, Edmund. *Man in Modern Fiction.* New York: Random House,
    1949.

Hanna, Charles B. *The Face of the Deep.* Philadelphia: Westminster
    Press, 1967.

Hesse, Hermann. *Demian.* New York: Harper & Row, 1965.

Howe, E. Graham, and Le Mesurier, L. *The Open Way.* London: Vincent
    Stuart & John M. Watkins, Ltd., 1939.

Jung, Carl G. *Collected Works.* Edited by G. Adler et al. Translated by R.

F. Hull 20 vols. 2d ed. Princeton, New Jersey: Princeton University
Press, 1968.

Krishnamurti, Jiddu. *Think on These Things.* New York: Harper
& Row, 1964.

Lynch, William F. *Images of Hope.* New York: New American
Library, Mentor, 1966.

Maslow, Abraham H. *Toward a Psychology of Being.* New York:
Van Nostrand-Reinhold, 1962.

Merton, Thomas. *No Man Is an Island.* New York: Doubleday, 1967.

Nietzsche, Friedrich. *Thus Spoke Zarathustra.* Translated by
R. J. Hollingdale. Baltimore, Md.: Penguin Books, 1961.

O'Connor, Elizabeth. *Journey Inward, Journey Outward.* New York:
Harper & Row, 1968.

——— *Our Many Selves.* New York: Harper & Row, 1971.

——— *Search for Silence.* Waco. Tex.: Word Books, 1972.

O'Connor, Flannery. *Mystery and Manners.* New York: Farrar, Straus &
Giroux, 1957.

Prather, Hugh. *Notes to Myself.* Lafayette, Cal.: Real People Press, 1970.

Richards, Mary Caroline. *Centering in Pottery, Poetry, and the Person.*
Middletown, Conn.: Wesleyan University Press, 1964.

Rilke, Rainer Maria. *Letters to a Young Poet.* Translated by M.D.
Herter Norton. New York: W. W. Norton & Co., 1934.

Rogers, Raymond. *Coming into Existence: The Struggle to Become an
Individual.* Cleveland, Ohio: World Publishing Co., 1967.

Saint-Exupery, Antoine de. *Wind, Sand and Stars.* Translated by Lewis
Galantuie. New York: Reynal & Hitchcock, 1939.

Shahn, Ben. *The Shape of Content.* Cambridge, Mass.: Harvard University
Press, 1957. (also in Vintage Books, paperback edition)

Thoreau, Henry David. *Walden and the Famous Essay on Civil
Disobedience.* New York: New American Library.

Tomkins, Calvin. *Eric Hoffer, An American Odyssey.* New York: E. P.
Dutton & Co., 1968.

Von Franz, Marie-Louise. *Interpretation of Fairytales.* New York:
Spring Publications, 1970.

Wickes, Frances G. *The Inner World of Choice.* New York: Harper & Row,
1963.

BOOKLETS AND PERIODICALS

Eversole, Finley. "The Politics of Creativity." *Journal of the Creative Society,* June 1969.

Hall, Mary Harrington. "A Conversation with Peter F. Drucker." *Psychology Today,* March 1968.

Phillips, Bernard. *The Search Will Make You Free.* Friends Conference on Religion and Psychology.

Special acknowledgment is made to the following who have granted permission for the reprinting of copyrighted material from the books and periodicals listed below:

GARNSTONE PRESS
The Divine and the Human, by Nicolas Berdyaev, copyright 1949 by Geoffrey Bles, Ltd.

GEORGE ALLEN & UNWIN LTD.
Understanding Human Nature, by Alfred Adler.

HARCOURT BRACE JOVANOVICH, INC.
No Man Is an Island, by Thomas Merton, copyright 1955 by The Abbey of Our Lady of Gethsemanie.
"Walls," by Constantine P. Cavafy. Reprinted from *The Complete Poems of Cavafy*, translated by Rae Dalven. Copyright 1949 by Rae Dalven.
Wind, Sand and Stars, by Antoine de Saint-Exupery.

HARPER & ROW, PUBLISHERS, INC.
Demian, by Hermann Hesse, pp. 98-99. (hardbound edition) *Eclipse of God*, by Martin Buber, p. 81.
Meister Eckhart: A Modern Translation, by Raymond Bernard Blakney.

The Inner World of Choice, by Frances G. Wickes, pp. 53, 64-65.
Think on These Things, by J. Krishnamurti, edited by D. Rajagopal, pp. 89,155,40,47,52-53.

HARVARD UNIVERSITY PRESS
The Shape of Content, by Ben Shahn.

HUMANITIES PRESS, INC., New York
Understanding Human Nature, by Alfred Adler.

THE MACMILLAN COMPANY
Between Man and Man, by Martin Buber, copyright 1965.

Printed in the United States
130028LV00002B/536/A

9 781928 717157